CODE CRAFTING: THE COMPLETE GUIDE TO MODERN PROGRAMMING LANGUAGES

Master Python, JavaScript, C++, and More for 2025 and Beyond

THOMPSON CARTER

TABLE OF CONTENTS

Introduction

Mastering Modern Programming Languages

In the ever-changing world of software development, one thing remains constant: the need for versatile, adaptable programmers who can master a wide range of programming languages and technologies. As technology continues to evolve at a rapid pace, the ability to stay ahead of the curve and continuously learn is essential for any developer who aims to remain relevant in the field. "Mastering Modern Programming Languages" is a comprehensive guide designed to equip you with the knowledge and skills to navigate the diverse landscape of programming languages and frameworks.

This book delves into the core programming languages that dominate the software development world today—**Python**, **JavaScript**, and **C++**—and explores the future of these languages and the trends shaping the industry. Whether you're just starting your programming journey or you're looking to deepen your understanding of these popular languages, this book provides you with the tools you need to succeed.

Why This Book?

As a developer, learning multiple programming languages is no longer a luxury but a necessity. Each language has its own strengths, weaknesses, and use cases, and the most successful developers know how to choose the right language for the right job. This book goes beyond simply teaching syntax and basic concepts; it focuses on real-world applications, best practices, and the evolving trends that are shaping the future of programming.

Throughout this book, you'll explore the strengths of each language, learn how to apply them in real-world projects, and gain insights into how the industry is evolving with the rise of **AI**, **IoT**, **Blockchain**, and **cloud-native development**. Additionally, we'll discuss how to stay updated with the latest programming trends, ensuring you remain at the forefront of the industry.

What You'll Learn in This Book

1. **Mastering Core Programming Languages**:
   - We'll start by diving deep into **Python**, **JavaScript**, and **C++**, covering everything from basic syntax to advanced features. You'll learn the ins and outs of each language, including best practices for writing efficient, maintainable code.
   - Explore the unique advantages and use cases of each language:

- **Python**: Used extensively in **data science, machine learning, web development**, and **automation**.
- **JavaScript**: The backbone of **web development** and the **browser**. JavaScript's versatility extends beyond the frontend, powering backend services and mobile apps through frameworks like **Node.js** and **React Native**.
- **C++**: Known for its **performance, memory management**, and **low-level control**, C++ is the language of choice for **systems programming, game development**, and **high-performance applications**.

2. **Future Trends in Programming**:
   - The landscape of programming languages is shifting rapidly, and we'll explore the emerging languages and paradigms shaping the future. Learn how **AI, machine learning, IoT**, and **Blockchain** are driving demand for new tools and frameworks.
   - Understand the increasing importance of **serverless computing, cloud development**, and **cross-platform mobile app development**, and

how these trends influence the languages developers should prioritize.

3. **Practical, Real-World Examples**:

    o Each chapter features **real-world examples** and **hands-on exercises** that allow you to apply what you've learned in practical ways. From building **web applications** to working with **APIs**, you'll gain invaluable experience that will directly enhance your programming skills.

    o Learn how to **integrate native features** like GPS, camera access, and storage in mobile apps, and explore how cutting-edge technologies like **cloud development** and **serverless architectures** are transforming the way we build applications.

4. **Learning from Industry Experts**:

    o Throughout this book, you'll find tips and advice from seasoned developers who have worked with these languages in real-world scenarios. These insights will help you understand how to approach complex problems, debug effectively, and write clean, maintainable code.

    o Learn how to stay updated with evolving language features, explore new technologies, and continue improving your skills beyond the book.

5. **Building a Versatile Skillset**:
   - This book emphasizes the importance of being a **versatile programmer**. By mastering **multiple programming languages**, you'll be equipped to handle a wide range of development tasks, from backend services and cloud computing to mobile app development and embedded systems.
   - Embrace the mindset of a **lifelong learner**—an essential trait for any modern programmer. This book provides you with the tools, knowledge, and resources to keep learning and adapting as new languages and technologies emerge.

Who Is This Book For?

This book is designed for both **beginner and intermediate developers** who want to expand their knowledge of modern programming languages and keep up with industry trends. Whether you're new to programming or already familiar with one or more languages, you'll find valuable insights, practical examples, and hands-on projects that will help you take your skills to the next level.

If you're a **Python developer** looking to branch out into **JavaScript** or **C++**, or a **JavaScript developer** wanting to understand the intricacies of backend development or performance optimization, this book is for you. Similarly, if you're an **experienced C++ developer** exploring new languages and modern programming trends, you'll find useful content to help you stay competitive in an ever-changing tech landscape.

What You Can Expect from This Book

By the end of this book, you will:

- Have a solid understanding of the core features, best practices, and advanced concepts of **Python**, **JavaScript**, and **C++**.
- Be able to apply these languages to build real-world applications, including web apps, mobile apps, and performance-critical systems.
- Gain an understanding of emerging programming trends like **AI**, **Blockchain**, and **IoT**, and how these trends are influencing the future of programming languages.
- Be equipped with the knowledge to stay updated on language features, industry developments, and emerging technologies.

- Be prepared to adapt to new languages and tools, ensuring you remain a versatile and capable developer for years to come.

Why Learning Multiple Languages Matters

In today's software development world, **versatility** is one of the most important traits a developer can have. The rise of **cloud computing**, **AI**, **IoT**, and **mobile applications** requires developers to master a diverse set of tools and technologies. While it's important to specialize in certain areas, learning multiple languages allows you to:

- **Choose the best tool for the job**: Different languages excel in different areas, and knowing multiple languages helps you choose the right one based on the project's needs.
- **Expand your career opportunities**: Companies look for developers who are adaptable and can work across various platforms and environments.
- **Stay ahead of industry trends**: The technology landscape is evolving quickly. Being proficient in multiple languages allows you to adapt to new trends and technologies faster.

Final Thoughts

"Mastering Modern Programming Languages" is more than just a guide to learning syntax and concepts; it is a roadmap to becoming a **versatile, future-ready developer**. As programming continues to evolve with new languages, frameworks, and technologies, this book will help you not only learn core languages like **Python**, **JavaScript**, and **C++** but also stay at the forefront of new developments in the industry.

Whether you are working on **web development**, **machine learning**, **cloud-based applications**, or **mobile app development**, this book will provide you with the skills and knowledge to confidently build high-quality, modern applications in today's fast-paced tech world. By the end, you'll be well on your way to becoming a **master of modern programming languages**, ready to tackle any challenge and adapt to the exciting technologies of the future.

Chapter 1: Introduction to Modern Programming Languages

Understanding the Role of Programming Languages in Today's Technology Landscape

In today's rapidly advancing digital world, programming languages are the foundation of nearly every piece of software, application, and system that drives our modern technology landscape. Whether it's web development, mobile applications, artificial intelligence, cloud computing, or data science, programming languages enable developers to create and implement solutions that impact every sector of the global economy. In essence, programming languages are the tools that translate human ideas and problem-solving strategies into executable software that drives innovation.

The digital world is becoming more complex by the day, and the need for software developers proficient in multiple languages is higher than ever. No single programming language is perfect for every task—each has its strengths, weaknesses, and niche applications. As the technology landscape diversifies, so too does the demand for developers who can choose the right tools for the job, switch between languages, and combine them effectively to build robust, scalable, and efficient solutions.

Programming languages play a critical role in shaping how applications and systems are developed, maintained, and evolved.

They impact factors such as code efficiency, speed, scalability, ease of use, and the ability to integrate with other technologies. Whether building a mobile app, developing a website, or creating an AI model, mastering multiple languages allows developers to be flexible, solve a wider range of problems, and create more powerful and versatile applications.

The Evolution of Programming Languages and the Importance of Mastering Multiple Languages

The history of programming languages traces the evolution of human understanding of computational problems and how best to solve them. Early programming languages, like ***Fortran*** and ***COBOL***, were designed to handle specific types of problems, such as scientific calculations or business data processing. These early languages were often low-level, meaning they were closer to machine code and thus harder for humans to work with.

As technology advanced, higher-level languages like ***C***, ***Java***, and ***Python*** were developed. These languages provided developers with more abstract and user-friendly ways to express logic and functionality, allowing for faster development times and easier maintenance. For instance, Python's clean and readable syntax has made it incredibly popular in areas such as web development, data science, and machine learning. JavaScript, on the other hand, revolutionized web development by allowing developers to create interactive, dynamic web pages.

Today, programming languages continue to evolve in response to new technological challenges and opportunities. In 2025, we see languages like *Python*, *JavaScript*, *C++*, and others evolving to meet the demands of AI, big data, and cloud-based systems. As the technology landscape becomes more interconnected, there is also a growing need for polyglot developers—those who are proficient in several programming languages—because they can leverage the strengths of each language depending on the task at hand.

Mastering multiple programming languages is no longer just a nice-to-have skill—it's essential for staying competitive in the tech industry. Each language has its own ecosystem, community, and best practices, offering unique features that make it the best choice for certain applications. By becoming proficient in a variety of languages, developers can choose the right tools for the job and become more versatile problem solvers.

Overview of Python, JavaScript, C++, and Other Key Languages in 2025

- **Python**: As one of the most popular programming languages in the world, Python has continued to thrive due to its simplicity, readability, and versatility. In 2025, Python is widely used in data science, machine learning, web development, automation, and scientific computing. Python's rich ecosystem of libraries and frameworks (like *Django*, *Flask*, *TensorFlow*, and *Pandas*) make it a go-to language for handling complex tasks in areas like AI and data analysis. Its ease of use and broad community support ensure it will remain a dominant language for years to come.

- **JavaScript**: JavaScript is the language of the web, powering interactive websites and dynamic user interfaces. In 2025, JavaScript continues to be the primary language for front-end web development, with frameworks like *React*, *Angular*, and *Vue.js* enabling developers to build robust, interactive web applications. JavaScript is also widely used on the server side through Node.js, making it a full-stack development language that can handle both client-side and server-side operations. The language's ever-growing ecosystem, combined with its ubiquity on the web, ensures its continued relevance.

- **C++**: C++ remains a critical language for performance-intensive applications, such as game development, systems programming, and applications that require direct hardware access. In 2025, C++ is still favored for its speed, control over memory, and compatibility with a wide range of hardware platforms. Modern versions of C++ (like C++17 and C++20) introduce advanced features, such as smart pointers, lambdas, and concurrency, that make C++ a powerful tool for creating high-performance applications. For developers working on projects where efficiency is paramount, C++ is still an indispensable language.

- **Other Key Languages**:
  - ○ **Java**: Java is widely used for enterprise applications, mobile apps (Android), and web applications. It remains one of the most robust and widely-used languages in large-scale systems development.
  - ○ **Rust**: Rust has been gaining traction due to its memory safety features and its performance capabilities. It is favored by developers working on system-level programming where safety and speed are critical.
  - ○ **Go (Golang)**: Go continues to be popular for backend development, especially in cloud-native applications and microservices. Known for its simplicity and efficiency, Go excels in handling high-concurrency applications.

Each of these languages plays a crucial role in 2025's technological landscape. Mastering Python, JavaScript, C++, and others will allow developers to stay competitive by providing them with the tools to build a wide range of applications, from simple websites to complex machine learning models.

How to Choose the Right Programming Language for Your Project

Choosing the right programming language for a project can be a challenging decision, as it requires balancing the project's requirements with the features and strengths of the available languages. Several factors should influence your decision, including:

- **Project Type**: Different languages excel in different domains. For example, Python is an excellent choice for data science, machine learning, and web applications, while C++ is ideal for high-performance applications such as games or operating systems. JavaScript is necessary for web development, particularly for building interactive websites and web applications.

- **Performance Requirements**: If your project demands high-performance computing or real-time execution (like video games or real-time simulations), C++ might be your best choice due to its speed and direct access to system resources. On the other hand, Python and JavaScript are generally slower but offer fast development cycles and ease of use.

- **Scalability and Maintenance**: Consider how well the language scales with your project. JavaScript, with its rich ecosystem, is great for scalable web applications. Python is popular for its ability to handle large datasets and integrate with other technologies, but C++ often shines when building systems that need to perform at scale without sacrificing performance.

- **Learning Curve**: Some languages, such as Python, have a gentle learning curve and are great for beginners. JavaScript is also beginner-friendly, especially for web development. C++ has a steeper learning curve due to its complexity and low-level features, but it offers unmatched performance control.

- **Community and Ecosystem**: A strong community and rich ecosystem can make a big difference when choosing a language. Python, JavaScript, and C++ all boast extensive libraries, frameworks, and community support, making it easier for developers to solve problems, find tutorials, and leverage existing tools for their projects.

By considering these factors, you can choose the language best suited to the project at hand. For many projects, developers may end up using more than one language to take advantage of the strengths of each, particularly when combining web development, data analysis, and systems programming.

Real-World Examples of Projects that Use Multiple Programming Languages

In the real world, developers rarely limit themselves to using just one programming language. Many successful projects leverage multiple languages to take advantage of the unique strengths of each. Here are a few examples:

- **Web Development**: Modern web applications often rely on JavaScript (for the front-end) and Python or Node.js (for the back-end). A popular example is a web application built with React (JavaScript) on the front-end and Django (Python) on the back-end. This combination allows for rapid development of dynamic, interactive websites while leveraging Python's strengths in handling data and complex logic on the server side.

- **Machine Learning and Web Applications**: A project like a recommendation engine for an e-commerce site might combine Python (using machine learning libraries like TensorFlow or Scikit-learn) with JavaScript (for the website's front-end and user interface). Python can be used for data processing, training models, and making predictions, while JavaScript can provide a seamless user experience by displaying recommendations in real-time.

- **Gaming**: In game development, C++ is often used to handle the game's core logic and performance-critical features, while Python might be used for scripting and prototyping. A popular game engine like Unreal Engine uses C++ to handle graphics rendering and physics, while Python can be used to create in-game content or automate tasks in the development pipeline.

- **IoT Systems**: In Internet of Things (IoT) applications, developers often use C++ for performance-critical embedded systems and Python for data processing and cloud integration. For instance, a smart home system might use C++ to manage sensors and devices locally, while Python runs on the server to aggregate and analyze the data in real-time.

These examples show how combining different programming languages can enable developers to build more efficient, scalable, and feature-rich applications.

Summary

The world of programming languages is diverse and constantly evolving. In 2025 and beyond, Python, JavaScript, C++, and other languages will continue to play pivotal roles in the development of software across various industries. By mastering multiple languages, developers can unlock new opportunities to build better, more innovative solutions. Choosing the right language for a project is crucial to its success, and in many cases, using more than one language will lead to the most powerful and efficient result. This book will guide you through these languages, providing the skills and knowledge needed to succeed in the modern programming landscape.

Chapter 2: Understanding Variables, Data Types, and Operators

Basic Python Data Types: Integers, Floats, Strings, and Booleans

In any programming language, understanding the core data types is foundational. In Python, there are four basic data types that every programmer must become familiar with: **integers**, **floats**, **strings**, and **booleans**. These data types form the building blocks of any Python program, allowing you to store, manipulate, and process different kinds of information.

- **Integers (int):**
    - Integers are whole numbers, both positive and negative, without decimal points. In Python, integers are represented with the `int` class.
    - Example: `5`, `-42`, `1000`.
    - Integers can be used for counting, indexing, and any situation that requires whole numbers.
    - Example:

    ```python
    age = 25  # an integer
    ```

- **Floats (float):**

o Floats are numbers that include decimal points.
   They are used for representing real numbers or
   continuous values. In Python, floats are
   represented with the `float` class.

o Example: `3.14`, `-0.001`, `2.0`.

o Floats are ideal for precision and calculations
   that require decimals, such as measurements
   or financial calculations.

o Example:

```python
price = 19.99  # a float
```

- **Strings (str):**

  o Strings are sequences of characters enclosed in
     either single quotes (' ') or double quotes (" "). In
     Python, strings are used to represent textual
     data, such as words, sentences, or any
     sequence of characters.

  o Example: `'Hello, World!'`, `"Python Programming"`, `'12345'` (which is treated as a
     string, not an integer).

  o Strings in Python are versatile and come with a
     variety of built-in methods to manipulate them

(e.g., changing case, splitting, replacing characters).

o Example:

```python
greeting = "Hello, World!"  # a string
```

- **Booleans (bool):**
  o Booleans represent one of two values: `True` or `False`. These values are used to represent logical states and are crucial for decision-making in your programs. They are typically the result of comparison operations or logical expressions.
  o Example: `True`, `False`.
  o Booleans are essential for control flow, such as in `if` statements or loops, where certain actions are taken based on conditions being true or false.
  o Example:

```python
is_raining = True  # a boolean value
```

Each of these basic data types is integral to writing effective Python code. They allow you to store different kinds of information and interact with it in meaningful ways.

Working with Variables and Understanding Scope

In Python, a **variable** is a symbolic name attached to a value. Variables allow you to store information that can be referenced and manipulated throughout your program. Python uses dynamic typing, which means you don't need to declare a variable's type explicitly; the interpreter automatically determines the type based on the assigned value.

- **Assigning Values to Variables**:
    - In Python, you simply assign a value to a variable using the = operator.
    - Example:

```python
python

age = 30
name = "Alice"
is_adult = True
```

- **Understanding Variable Scope**:
    - **Global Scope**: A variable defined outside any function is in the global scope. It is accessible throughout the program.

python

```python
global_var = 100   # Global variable

def print_var():
    print(global_var)   # Accessible in the
function

print_var()   # Output: 100
```

- **Local Scope**: Variables defined within a function are local to that function. They are not accessible outside the function.

python

```python
def my_function():
    local_var = 50   # Local variable
    print(local_var)

my_function()   # Output: 50
print(local_var)       #  Error:  NameError,
local_var  is  not  defined  outside  the
function
```

- **Modifying Variables**:
  - Variables can be reassigned or modified during the execution of a program. The new value can

be of any type, and Python will handle the type conversion for you.

o Example:

```python

x = 10
x = x + 5   # Reassign x with a new value
(15)
print(x)   # Output: 15
```

Common Python Operators (Arithmetic, Logical, Comparison, etc.)

Operators in Python are symbols that perform operations on variables or values. Python provides several types of operators that allow you to manipulate variables and data in various ways. Let's take a look at the most commonly used operators:

- **Arithmetic Operators**: These operators perform mathematical calculations.
  - o + (addition)
  - o - (subtraction)
  - o * (multiplication)
  - o / (division)
  - o // (floor division, which discards the decimal part)
  - o % (modulus, which returns the remainder)

o ** (exponentiation)

Example:

python

```
x = 10
y = 3

print(x + y)    # Output: 13
print(x - y)    # Output: 7
print(x * y)    # Output: 30
print(x / y)    # Output: 3.3333333333333335
print(x // y)   # Output: 3
print(x % y)    #' Output: 1
print(x ** y)   # Output: 1000
```

- **Comparison Operators**: These operators are used to compare two values and return a boolean (True or False).
    - o == (equal to)
    - o != (not equal to)
    - o > (greater than)
    - o < (less than)
    - o >= (greater than or equal to)
    - o <= (less than or equal to)

Example:

python

```
a = 10
b = 20

print(a == b)    # Output: False
print(a != b)    # Output: True
print(a > b)     # Output: False
print(a < b)     # Output: True
print(a >= b)    # Output: False
print(a <= b)    # Output: True
```

- **Logical Operators**: Logical operators are used to combine multiple conditions.
    - and (returns True if both conditions are true)
    - or (returns True if at least one condition is true)
    - not (returns the inverse boolean value)

Example:

python

```
x = 5
y = 10

print(x > 0 and y < 20)    # Output: True
print(x > 0 or y > 20)     # Output: True
print(not (x > 0))         # Output: False
```

Real-World Examples: Simple Data Processing and Calculations

Now that we understand variables, data types, and operators, let's apply this knowledge to some real-world scenarios. These examples show how Python can be used for simple data processing and calculations, tasks that are often encountered in real applications.

- **Example 1: Simple Data Processing - Calculating the Average of a List**: Suppose we want to process a list of numbers and calculate their average.

  python

  ```python
  numbers = [10, 20, 30, 40, 50]
  total = sum(numbers)   # Add all numbers together
  count = len(numbers)   # Get the number of items
  in the list
  average = total / count  # Calculate the average
  print(f"The average is: {average}")   # Output:
  30.0
  ```

  In this example, we used the `sum()` function to calculate the total of the numbers in the list and the `len()` function to find the number of items. Then, we calculated the average by dividing the total by the count of numbers.

- **Example 2: Basic Calculation - Simple Interest**: Let's calculate the simple interest on a loan using the formula:

Simple Interest=P×R×T100\text{Simple Interest} = \frac{P \times R \times T}{100}Simple Interest=100P×R×T

Where P is the principal, R is the rate of interest, and T is the time in years.

```python
principal = 1000  # Principal amount
rate_of_interest = 5  # Rate of interest per year
time_in_years = 3  # Time in years

simple_interest = (principal * rate_of_interest
* time_in_years) / 100
total_amount = principal + simple_interest

print(f"The simple interest is:
{simple_interest}")  # Output: 150.0
print(f"The total amount to be paid is:
{total_amount}")  # Output: 1150.0
```

This example demonstrates how to calculate simple interest using the basic arithmetic operators and store the result in a variable for further processing.

Summary

In this chapter, we've covered the fundamental building blocks of Python programming: data types, variables, and operators. These concepts are the foundation upon which more complex programs and applications are built. With a solid understanding of these essentials, you're ready to move on to more advanced topics, such as control flow, functions, and object-oriented programming. By mastering these basic elements, you'll be able to write more efficient, readable, and functional code for a wide range of real-world applications.

Chapter 3: Control Flow and Loops in Python

If Statements, Loops, and Conditionals in Python

Control flow refers to the order in which individual statements, instructions, or function calls are executed or evaluated. In Python, control flow structures allow you to direct the execution of your program based on conditions or repetitive tasks. The two most common control structures are **if statements** and **loops**.

- **If Statements**:
    - o `if` statements allow you to execute a block of code only if a certain condition is true. This is the most fundamental control flow structure, allowing your program to make decisions.
    - o Syntax:

        ```python

        if condition:
            # Code to execute if condition is true
        ```

    - o You can extend an `if` statement with `elif` (else if) and `else` to check for multiple conditions.
    - o Example:

```python
x = 10
if x > 5:
    print("x is greater than 5")
else:
    print("x is less than or equal to 5")
# Output: x is greater than 5
```

- **Loops**:
  - **For Loops**: Used for iterating over a sequence (like a list, string, or range). The `for` loop allows you to repeat a block of code multiple times, once for each item in a sequence.
  - Syntax:

```python
for item in sequence:
    # Code to execute for each item
```

  - Example:

```python
for i in range(5):
    print(i)
# Output: 0, 1, 2, 3, 4 (each on a new line)
```

- **While Loops**: Continuously execute a block of code as long as the specified condition is true.
- Syntax:

```python

while condition:
    # Code to execute as long as condition
is true
```

- Example:

```python

i = 0
while i < 5:
    print(i)
    i += 1
# Output: 0, 1, 2, 3, 4 (each on a new line)
```

- **Break and Continue**:
  - The `break` statement is used to exit a loop early, regardless of the condition.
  - The `continue` statement skips the current iteration and moves on to the next one.
  - Example of `break`:

```python
```

```python
for i in range(10):
    if i == 5:
        break
    print(i)
# Output: 0, 1, 2, 3, 4
```

o **Example of** continue:

```python
python

for i in range(5):
    if i == 3:
        continue
    print(i)
# Output: 0, 1, 2, 4 (skips 3)
```

Understanding the Flow of Control in Python Programs

Control flow is crucial in Python programming as it determines the sequence of execution. You can control the path your program follows using if statements, loops, and other control structures. Here's a breakdown of how the flow of control works:

- **Conditionals**: When you use if, elif, and else statements, you're setting up conditions that the program will check during execution. If the condition is true, the program will execute the corresponding block of code. If it's false, the program will check the next condition or move to the else block (if provided).

Example:

python

```
age = 18
if age < 18:
    print("You are a minor.")
elif age == 18:
    print("You just turned 18!")
else:
    print("You are an adult.")
# Output: You just turned 18!
```

- **Loops**: Loops allow you to repeat a block of code. The flow of control will return to the top of the loop and continue until the condition (in a while loop) or the sequence (in a for loop) is exhausted.

Example:

python

```
fruits = ["apple", "banana", "cherry"]
for fruit in fruits:
    print(fruit)
# Output: apple, banana, cherry (each on a new
line)
```

In the case of the while loop, the program will continue executing as long as the condition remains true.

- **Flow of Control with Functions**: Functions in Python also affect the control flow by allowing you to group code into reusable blocks. The program will jump to the function definition when called, execute the code inside, and then return to where it left off after the function completes.

Real-World Example: A Python Script to Filter Data from a List

Let's look at a real-world example where we filter data based on a certain condition. For instance, suppose we have a list of ages, and we want to filter out only those ages that are 18 or older, as those individuals are eligible to vote.

- Example: Filter eligible voters from a list of ages

python

```python
ages = [12, 15, 18, 22, 25, 16, 30, 17]
eligible_voters = []

# Loop through the list and check if the age is 18 or older
for age in ages:
    if age >= 18:
        eligible_voters.append(age)

print("Eligible voters:", eligible_voters)
# Output: Eligible voters: [18, 22, 25, 30]
```

- **Explanation**: In this example:
    - We have a list called `ages`, which contains ages of various individuals.
    - We create an empty list `eligible_voters` to store the ages of those eligible to vote.
    - Using a `for` loop, we iterate over the `ages` list, and inside the loop, we use an `if` statement to check if each age is 18 or greater.
    - If the condition is true, we append the age to the `eligible_voters` list.
    - Finally, we print the list of eligible voters.

This example shows how control flow structures, such as loops and conditionals, work together to filter data from a list.

Best Practices for Writing Clean, Readable Code with Control Flow

When working with control flow in Python, it's important to follow best practices to ensure that your code is not only functional but also clean, readable, and maintainable.

1. **Use Meaningful Variable Names**:
    - Choose variable names that clearly describe their purpose. For example, `eligible_voters` is a descriptive name, whereas `ev` might be confusing.

2. **Indentation**:
   - Python relies on indentation to define code blocks. Always use consistent indentation (typically 4 spaces) to make the code easy to follow.

3. **Avoid Nested Loops and Conditionals**:
   - While sometimes necessary, deeply nested loops or conditionals can make code harder to read. If possible, refactor the code into smaller functions or use early returns to avoid excessive nesting.

4. **Comment Your Code**:
   - Although Python is known for its readable syntax, commenting your code can help others (and your future self) understand the purpose of the control flow structures you've used. Write comments explaining complex logic or the reason behind certain conditions.

5. **Break Long Functions or Loops into Smaller Parts**:
   - If a loop or `if` statement is getting too long, consider breaking the logic into smaller functions or using helper variables to clarify intent.

6. **Use List Comprehensions**:

o Python offers list comprehensions as a compact, elegant way to filter or transform lists. This can replace the need for many loops and `if` statements, making your code cleaner.

Example of list comprehension for filtering voters:

```python
```

```python
eligible_voters = [age for age in ages if age >= 18]
print("Eligible voters:", eligible_voters)
# Output: Eligible voters: [18, 22, 25, 30]
```

List comprehensions are efficient and often more readable when you need to apply a condition to every item in a sequence.

7. **Use `else` in Loops for Clarity**:

o Python's `else` statement can be used after loops and `if` statements to handle cases when the loop doesn't execute or the condition is not met. This can help make the flow of control clearer.

Example of using `else` with a loop:

```python
```

```python
for age in ages:
    if age >= 18:
        print(f"{age} is eligible to vote.")
        break
else:
    print("No eligible voters found.")
```

Summary

In this chapter, we've covered essential concepts of control flow in Python, including `if` statements, loops, and conditionals. These structures allow you to dictate the execution path of your program based on conditions, making your code dynamic and flexible. By understanding how to properly use control flow, you'll be able to build more complex and functional programs.

We also explored a real-world example of filtering data from a list and applying the right control flow structures to solve a common problem. Finally, following best practices for clean, readable code will ensure that your Python programs remain easy to understand and maintain, regardless of their complexity.

Chapter 4: Functions and Modules in Python

Defining and Calling Functions in Python

Functions are one of the most powerful tools in programming. They allow you to organize your code, reuse logic, and simplify complex tasks. In Python, defining and calling functions is straightforward. A function is essentially a block of code that only runs when it is called. Functions help break down your program into smaller, manageable parts.

- **Defining a Function**:
    - In Python, you define a function using the `def` keyword, followed by the function name and parentheses. If your function takes any parameters (also called arguments), they go inside the parentheses.
    - Syntax:

        ```python
        def function_name(parameters):
            # Code block
            return result  # Optional
        ```

    - Example:

```python
python

def greet(name):
    print(f"Hello, {name}!")
```

- **Calling a Function**:
    - o To call a function, simply use its name followed by parentheses. If the function expects arguments, you pass the required values inside the parentheses.
    - o Example:

```python
python

greet("Alice")   # Output: Hello, Alice!
```

Functions allow you to encapsulate logic that can be reused throughout your program. This reduces redundancy and makes your code more readable and maintainable.

Passing Arguments, Returning Values, and Understanding Scope

- **Passing Arguments**:
    - o Arguments (or parameters) are values passed to a function when it is called. These allow you to send information to the function, enabling it to perform specific tasks.

- Functions can accept different types of arguments:
  - **Positional arguments**: The values are assigned based on the order in which they are passed.
  - **Keyword arguments**: Arguments passed by explicitly specifying the parameter name.
- Example:

python

```python
def greet(name, message="Hello"):
    print(f"{message}, {name}!")

greet("Alice")   # Output: Hello, Alice!
greet("Bob", "Good morning")   # Output:
Good morning, Bob!
```

- **Returning Values**:
  - Functions can return a value using the `return` statement. This allows you to send a result back to the calling code, which can then be used further.
  - Example:

python

```
def add(a, b):
    return a + b

result = add(5, 3)
print(result)   # Output: 8
```

- **Understanding Scope**:
  - **Local scope**: Variables defined inside a function are local to that function and cannot be accessed outside it.
  - **Global scope**: Variables defined outside of any function are global and can be accessed anywhere in the program.
  - Example of local scope:

    python

    ```
    def my_function():
        local_var = "I'm local"
        print(local_var)

    my_function()   # Output: I'm local
    print(local_var)   # Error: NameError
    ```

  - Example of global scope:

    python

```python
global_var = "I'm global"

def print_global():
    print(global_var)

print_global()  # Output: I'm global
```

Understanding scope is important for managing the visibility of variables and ensuring that your functions have the right access to data.

Organizing Code with Python Modules

As your Python programs grow, it becomes crucial to keep your code organized and modular. **Modules** are simply Python files that contain functions, variables, and other definitions that you can reuse in different parts of your program or across multiple projects.

- **Creating a Module**:
  - To create a module, simply write a Python file with the desired functions and variables.
  - Example: `my_module.py`

    ```python
    python

    def add(a, b):
        return a + b

    def subtract(a, b):
        return a - b
    ```

- **Using a Module**:
  - To use the code in a module, you import it using the `import` statement.
  - Example:

```python
import my_module

result = my_module.add(5, 3)
print(result)   # Output: 8
```

- **Importing Specific Functions**:
  - Instead of importing the entire module, you can import only specific functions from a module to keep your code clean and efficient.
  - Example:

```python
from my_module import add

result = add(10, 5)
print(result)   # Output: 15
```

- **Organizing Large Programs**:
  - As your projects grow, you can organize them into multiple files (modules) and directories.

Python allows you to group modules into packages (a folder with an `__init__.py` file), making your code even more modular and easier to maintain.

Real-World Example: Building a Python Application that Interacts with an API

In this section, we'll demonstrate how to build a simple Python application that interacts with an external API to fetch and display data. For this example, we'll use the **Requests** library to interact with a public API that provides JSON data.

1. **Install the Requests Library**: To install the Requests library, use `pip`:

   bash

   ```
   pip install requests
   ```

2. **Building the Application**: We will create a function to fetch data from a public API (e.g., the JSONPlaceholder API), process the data, and display it in a user-friendly format.

   Example:

   python

   ```
   import requests
   ```

```python
def fetch_user_data(user_id):
    url = f"https://jsonplaceholder.typicode.com/users/{user_id}"
    response = requests.get(url)
    if response.status_code == 200:
        return response.json()   # Return JSON data
    else:
        print("Failed to retrieve data")
        return None

def display_user_info(user_id):
    user_data = fetch_user_data(user_id)
    if user_data:
        print(f"Name: {user_data['name']}")
        print(f"Email: {user_data['email']}")
        print(f"City: {user_data['address']['city']}")
    else:
        print("No data available.")

# Call the function to display user info for user with ID 1
display_user_info(1)
```

Explanation:

- o `fetch_user_data(user_id)` **fetches data from the API using the** `requests.get()` **method. If the** request is successful (status code 200), it returns the response as a JSON object.

- o `display_user_info(user_id)` calls `fetch_user_data()` to retrieve the user data and prints the name, email, and city of the user in a readable format.

Output (example):

```makefile
makefile


Name: Leanne Graham
Email: Sincere@april.biz
City: Gwenborough
```

This real-world example demonstrates how functions can interact with external data sources (APIs) to provide dynamic content. The modularization of fetching and displaying data in separate functions also shows how you can organize your code for better readability and reusability.

Practical Tips for Code Reuse and Modularization

1. **Avoid Repeating Code**:
   - o Functions allow you to reuse code by encapsulating repeated logic. This makes your code more efficient and easier to maintain.

o Instead of repeating the same logic, wrap it in a function and call it whenever needed.

2. **Keep Functions Focused**:

   o Functions should do one thing and do it well. This makes them more predictable and easier to test.

   o Example: Instead of creating a function that handles both user input and data processing, split them into separate functions.

3. **Use Default Arguments**:

   o Use default values for function parameters when appropriate. This reduces the need for explicit arguments, making your functions more flexible.

   o Example:

```python
def greet(name="Guest"):
    print(f"Hello, {name}!")
```

4. **Document Your Functions**:

   o Always add docstrings to your functions. A well-written docstring describes what the function does, its parameters, and its return value. This improves code readability and helps others understand your code.

o Example:

```python

def add(a, b):
    """
    Adds two numbers and returns the result.

    Parameters:
    a (int or float): The first number.
    b (int or float): The second number.

    Returns:
    int or float: The sum of a and b.
    """
    return a + b
```

5. **Group Related Functions into Modules**:

o As your program grows, organize functions into modules (separate Python files). This makes your codebase easier to manage and scale.

o For example, if you're working on a game, you might have modules for graphics (`graphics.py`), user input (`input.py`), and game logic (`game_logic.py`).

6. **Testing and Error Handling**:
   - Ensure that your functions are resilient by adding error handling (e.g., try-except blocks) to handle unexpected inputs or failures (such as API requests failing).
   - Write unit tests to ensure your functions behave as expected, especially when working with external resources.

Summary

In this chapter, we covered how to define and call functions in Python, as well as how to pass arguments, return values, and manage scope. Functions are essential for breaking your code into reusable, manageable pieces, making your code more efficient and maintainable. We also learned how to organize our code into Python modules for better modularization, enabling code reuse across different projects. Finally, we applied our knowledge to build a Python application that interacts with an API, demonstrating how functions can be used to integrate external data into your programs. By mastering functions and modules, you'll be able to write clean, efficient, and maintainable Python code.

Chapter 5: Object-Oriented Programming in Python

Introduction to Classes and Objects in Python

Object-Oriented Programming (OOP) is a programming paradigm that organizes software design around data, or objects, rather than functions and logic. In Python, OOP is a powerful way to structure your code, making it more modular, reusable, and easier to maintain. In OOP, everything is an object, and objects are instances of classes. A **class** serves as a blueprint for creating objects, while an **object** is an instance of a class with specific attributes and behaviors.

- **Classes**:
    - A class defines the properties (attributes) and methods (functions) that the objects created from the class will have.
    - You define a class using the `class` keyword, followed by the class name and a colon. Inside the class, you define methods and properties using standard Python syntax.

Example:

```python

class Dog:
```

```python
def __init__(self, name, age):
    self.name = name   # Attribute
    self.age = age     # Attribute

def bark(self):   # Method
    print(f"{self.name} says Woof!")
```

- **Objects**:
    - Objects are instances of a class. You create an object by calling the class as if it were a function and passing arguments to the class constructor (__init__ method).
    - Example of creating an object:

    python

    ```python
    my_dog = Dog("Buddy", 3)
    my_dog.bark()   # Output: Buddy says Woof!
    ```

In this example, Dog is a class, and my_dog is an object (instance) of the Dog class. The __init__ method initializes the object's attributes, and bark() is a method that defines the behavior of the Dog object.

Understanding Inheritance, Encapsulation, and Polymorphism
Object-Oriented Programming is based on several core principles that enable developers to build more flexible and scalable systems. The three most important concepts in OOP are **inheritance**, **encapsulation**, and **polymorphism**.

- **Inheritance**:
  - ○ Inheritance allows one class (child class) to inherit the properties and methods of another class (parent class). This helps avoid code duplication and promotes reusability. The child class can also add its own unique attributes or methods.
  - ○ Example:

python

```python
class Animal:
    def __init__(self, name):
        self.name = name

    def speak(self):
        print(f"{self.name}     makes     a
sound.")

class Dog(Animal):  # Dog inherits from
Animal
    def __init__(self, name, breed):
        super().__init__(name)  # Call the
parent class constructor
        self.breed = breed

    def speak(self):  # Override the speak
method
        print(f"{self.name} barks.")
```

```
# Create objects
animal = Animal("Generic Animal")
dog = Dog("Buddy", "Golden Retriever")

animal.speak()    # Output: Generic Animal
makes a sound.
dog.speak()       # Output: Buddy barks.
```

- In this example, Dog inherits from Animal. It inherits the __init__ and speak methods, but the speak method is overridden in the Dog class to provide specific behavior for dogs.

- **Encapsulation**:
    - Encapsulation is the concept of restricting access to some of an object's attributes or methods, providing a controlled interface for interacting with them. This helps protect data integrity and hides internal implementation details.
    - In Python, you can use the underscore (_) to indicate a protected variable, and double underscore (__) to indicate a private variable.
    - Example:

    python

```
class Account:
    def __init__(self, balance):
        self.__balance = balance  # Private
attribute

    def deposit(self, amount):
        if amount > 0:
            self.__balance += amount

    def get_balance(self):
        return self.__balance

acc = Account(100)
acc.deposit(50)
print(acc.get_balance())   # Output: 150
#   print(acc.__balance)        #    Error:
AttributeError
```

- In this example, the __balance attribute is private, meaning it cannot be accessed directly outside the class. Instead, you interact with it using the deposit() method and the get_balance() method.

- **Polymorphism**:

  o Polymorphism allows different classes to define methods with the same name, but with different behaviors. This enables objects from different classes to be treated as objects of a common superclass, allowing for flexible and interchangeable code.

o Example:

```python
python

class Cat(Animal):
    def speak(self):
        print(f"{self.name} meows.")

# Create objects
cat = Cat("Whiskers")
dog = Dog("Buddy", "Beagle")

animals = [cat, dog]
for animal in animals:
    animal.speak()  # Each object will use
its own version of speak()
# Output:
# Whiskers meows.
# Buddy barks.
```

- Here, both Cat and Dog classes override the speak() method, but they implement their own specific behavior. The speak() method is polymorphic because the method behaves differently depending on the class of the object calling it.

Real-World Example: Building a Simple Inventory System in Python

Let's apply OOP principles to build a simple inventory system. In this system, we'll create classes for Item (a basic item in the inventory) and Inventory (which holds a collection of items).

1. **Define the Item Class**:
   - o The Item class will have attributes like name, quantity, and price. It will also have a method to display information about the item.
2. **Define the Inventory Class**:
   - o The Inventory class will manage a list of items, allowing you to add items, remove items, and display all items in the inventory.

python

```python
class Item:
    def __init__(self, name, quantity, price):
        self.name = name
        self.quantity = quantity
        self.price = price

    def display(self):
        print(f"{self.name}          -          Quantity:
{self.quantity}, Price: ${self.price:.2f}")

    def update_quantity(self, quantity):
        self.quantity += quantity
```

```python
class Inventory:
    def __init__(self):
        self.items = []

    def add_item(self, item):
        self.items.append(item)

    def remove_item(self, item_name):
        for item in self.items:
            if item.name == item_name:
                self.items.remove(item)
                print(f"{item_name}    removed    from
inventory.")
                return
        print(f"{item_name} not found in inventory.")

    def display_inventory(self):
        for item in self.items:
            item.display()

# Creating Items
item1 = Item("Laptop", 10, 799.99)
item2 = Item("Smartphone", 20, 499.99)

# Creating Inventory and adding items
inventory = Inventory()
inventory.add_item(item1)
inventory.add_item(item2)

# Displaying inventory
inventory.display_inventory()
```

```
# Updating item quantity
item1.update_quantity(5)

# Removing an item
inventory.remove_item("Smartphone")

# Displaying updated inventory
inventory.display_inventory()
```

Explanation:

- The `Item` class represents an item in the inventory, with attributes for `name`, `quantity`, and `price`. The method `display()` prints out the item details, and `update_quantity()` allows you to add or subtract from the item's quantity.
- The `Inventory` class holds a list of items and provides methods to add, remove, and display items.
- The program demonstrates how to interact with the inventory by adding items, displaying them, and updating or removing them.

Output Example:

```yaml
yaml

Laptop - Quantity: 10, Price: $799.99
Smartphone - Quantity: 20, Price: $499.99
```

```
Smartphone removed from inventory.
Laptop - Quantity: 15, Price: $799.99
```

How Object-Oriented Design Can Improve Code Quality and Maintainability

Object-Oriented Programming (OOP) can significantly improve the quality and maintainability of your code. Here's how:

- **Modularity**: By organizing code into classes, you make it more modular. Each class represents a self-contained unit with its own properties and behaviors. This makes it easier to manage and maintain different components of a program.
- **Reusability**: Once a class is defined, you can create multiple instances of it and reuse the logic throughout your program. Inheritance allows you to reuse and extend existing code without modifying the original class.
- **Maintainability**: When your code is well-structured using OOP principles, it becomes easier to understand, modify, and debug. Changes made to a class are automatically reflected in all instances of that class, reducing the likelihood of introducing bugs when making updates.
- **Scalability**: As your program grows, you can easily scale it by adding new classes and extending existing ones through inheritance. The use of polymorphism allows you to add new behaviors without changing existing code.

- **Encapsulation**: By hiding the internal workings of your classes (i.e., using private variables and methods), you reduce the risk of accidental interference from other parts of your code. This makes the system more robust and less error-prone.

Summary

In this chapter, we introduced the fundamentals of Object-Oriented Programming (OOP) in Python, including classes, objects, inheritance, encapsulation, and polymorphism. We demonstrated how these concepts can be applied in a real-world scenario by building a simple inventory system. By understanding and using OOP principles, you can create more modular, reusable, and maintainable Python programs. As you continue developing with Python, object-oriented design will become a valuable tool for structuring your code in a way that is both efficient and easy to maintain.

Chapter 6: Introduction to JavaScript

The Role of JavaScript in Modern Web Development

JavaScript is a cornerstone of modern web development. It is a high-level, interpreted programming language that enables developers to create dynamic, interactive websites and applications. Unlike HTML and CSS, which define the structure and style of a webpage, JavaScript is responsible for controlling the behavior and functionality of web pages. It's the programming language that brings websites to life, allowing developers to implement interactive features like:

- Form validation
- User interactions (e.g., clicks, hover effects)
- Real-time updates (e.g., live chat, live sports scores)
- Animations
- Fetching and displaying data from APIs without refreshing the page (commonly known as AJAX)

JavaScript is executed in the browser, which means it runs on the user's device rather than a server. This makes it ideal for creating responsive, fast, and interactive web experiences.

JavaScript is often used in combination with other technologies like HTML (for structure) and CSS (for styling) to create fully functional, interactive web applications. In addition to client-side development,

JavaScript has also become popular for server-side development with the advent of *Node.js*, which allows developers to run JavaScript on the server, enabling full-stack JavaScript development.

Setting Up Your JavaScript Environment and Writing Your First Program

To start working with JavaScript, you don't need to install any special software—your web browser already includes everything you need to run JavaScript. Every modern web browser (Chrome, Firefox, Safari, Edge) has a built-in JavaScript engine that can execute your code.

However, for writing and testing JavaScript, it's helpful to have an integrated development environment (IDE) or code editor. Some popular choices are:

- **Visual Studio Code (VSCode)**: A powerful, free code editor with JavaScript support.
- **Sublime Text**: A lightweight text editor for coding.
- **Atom**: A customizable open-source editor.

Once you've chosen an editor, you can write JavaScript code directly in an HTML file, or you can create a separate `.js` file. Let's start with the basics.

- **Writing Your First Program**: To write JavaScript code, you can create an HTML file and embed JavaScript within `<script>` tags, or create an external JavaScript file with a `.js` extension.

Example 1: Writing JavaScript in an HTML file:

html

```html
<!DOCTYPE html>
<html lang="en">
<head>
    <meta charset="UTF-8">
    <meta name="viewport" content="width=device-width,
initial-scale=1.0">
    <title>My First JavaScript Program</title>
</head>
<body>
    <h1>Welcome to JavaScript!</h1>

    <script>
        // JavaScript code inside the script tags
        alert("Hello,    World!    This    is    my    first
JavaScript program!");
    </script>
</body>
</html>
```

In this example:

- The JavaScript code is placed between `<script>` tags inside the HTML document.

- The `alert()` function is a built-in JavaScript function that displays a pop-up message in the browser.

- **Running the Program**: To run the program, simply save the file with a `.html` extension and open it in your web browser. You should see an alert pop-up with the message "Hello, World!"

- **Creating a Separate JavaScript File**: Alternatively, you can write JavaScript in an external file and link it to your HTML document. This is the recommended approach for larger projects.

Example 2: Using an external JavaScript file:

1. Create a `script.js` file:

```
javascript
```

```
// script.js file
alert("This is my first JavaScript program from
an external file!");
```

2. Link the `script.js` file to your HTML file:

```
html
```

```
<!DOCTYPE html>
<html lang="en">
<head>
    <meta charset="UTF-8">
```

```
    <meta name="viewport" content="width=device-
width, initial-scale=1.0">
    <title>External JavaScript Example</title>
</head>
<body>
    <h1>External JavaScript File</h1>

    <script src="script.js"></script> <!-- Link
to external JavaScript file -->
</body>
</html>
```

In this example, the JavaScript file (script.js) is loaded and executed within the HTML document, just like inline JavaScript, but it keeps the code separated and more organized.

Understanding JavaScript Syntax and Data Types

JavaScript syntax refers to the rules that govern how JavaScript code is written. Understanding the basic syntax and data types is crucial for writing JavaScript programs.

- **Variables**:
    - Variables are used to store data values. In JavaScript, you can define variables using let, const, or var.
        - let is used for variables that can change.
        - const is used for constants (values that won't change).

- var is an older keyword that is less commonly used now in modern JavaScript development.

Example:

```javascript
let name = "Alice";   // String variable
const age = 30;       // Constant variable
let isActive = true; // Boolean variable
```

- **Data Types**: JavaScript supports several data types, including:
  - **String**: Textual data, enclosed in quotes ("Hello" or 'World').
  - **Number**: Numeric values (both integers and floats) like 10 or 3.14.
  - **Boolean**: true or false.
  - **Object**: A collection of key-value pairs, often used to store structured data.
  - **Array**: A list-like collection of items.
  - **Undefined**: A variable that has been declared but not assigned a value.
  - **Null**: Represents the absence of any object value.

Example:

javascript

```
let firstName = "John";    // String
let age = 25;              // Number
let isStudent = true;      // Boolean
let user = { name: "John", age: 25 };   // Object
let numbers = [1, 2, 3, 4, 5];   // Array
let undefinedVar;          // Undefined
let emptyVar = null;       // Null
```

- **Operators**: JavaScript uses operators to perform operations on variables and values. These include:
    - **Arithmetic Operators** (+, -, *, /, %).
    - **Comparison Operators** (==, !=, >, <, >=, <=).
    - **Logical Operators** (&&, ||, !).
    - **Assignment Operators** (=, +=, -=, etc.).

Example:

javascript

```
let a = 10;
let b = 5;
let sum = a + b; // Arithmetic operator
console.log(sum); // Output: 15


let isEqual = (a == b); // Comparison operator
console.log(isEqual); // Output: false
```

```
let isTrue = (a > b) && (b > 0); // Logical
operator
console.log(isTrue); // Output: true
```

Real-World Example: A Simple Interactive Web Page Using JavaScript

Let's create a simple interactive web page using JavaScript. In this example, we'll create a button that, when clicked, changes the content of a paragraph on the webpage.

1. **HTML Structure**:

```html
html

<!DOCTYPE html>
<html lang="en">
<head>
    <meta charset="UTF-8">
    <meta name="viewport" content="width=device-width, initial-scale=1.0">
    <title>Interactive Web Page</title>
</head>
<body>
    <h1>Interactive Web Page with JavaScript</h1>
    <p id="message">Click the button to change this text.</p>
    <button id="changeTextBtn">Change Text</button>
```

```
<script src="script.js"></script> <!-- Link
to external JS file -->
</body>
</html>
```

2. **JavaScript Functionality (script.js)**:

```javascript

// Accessing elements from the HTML
const              button              =
document.getElementById("changeTextBtn");
const              message              =
document.getElementById("message");

// Adding an event listener to the button
button.addEventListener("click", function() {
    message.textContent = "The text has been
changed!";   // Change the paragraph text
});
```

Explanation:

- In this example:
    - We have an HTML button with the id `changeTextBtn` and a paragraph with the id `message`.
    - In the JavaScript file, we use `getElementById()` to access the button and paragraph elements.

- o We then attach a click event listener to the button, so when the button is clicked, the text of the paragraph changes.

Output:

- Initially, the paragraph says: "Click the button to change this text."
- After clicking the button, the text changes to: "The text has been changed!"

Summary

In this chapter, we introduced JavaScript, covering its essential role in modern web development and how it enables interactivity and dynamic functionality on webpages. We walked through setting up a JavaScript environment, writing basic code, understanding JavaScript syntax, and using variables and data types. Finally, we built a simple interactive web page that responds to user input. By mastering these basic concepts, you can begin exploring more advanced JavaScript features and techniques to enhance your web development skills.

Chapter 7: Working with Variables and Data Types in JavaScript

Understanding JavaScript's Primitive Data Types

In JavaScript, primitive data types represent simple values that are not objects and have no methods. These are the basic building blocks for variables and functions. JavaScript has six primitive data types:

1. **Number**:
   - Represents both integers and floating-point numbers.
   - Examples: `10`, `3.14`, `-100`, `2.5`

2. **String**:
   - Represents a sequence of characters enclosed in single or double quotes.
   - Examples: `'Hello'`, `"World"`, `'JavaScript'`

3. **Boolean**:
   - Represents a logical value, either `true` or `false`.
   - Examples: `true`, `false`

4. **Undefined**:
   - Represents a variable that has been declared but not assigned a value.
   - Example:

   ```javascript
   ```

```
let x;
console.log(x);   // Output: undefined
```

5. **Null**:

   o Represents the intentional absence of any object value. It is a special keyword.

   o Example:

   ```
   javascript
   ```

   ```
   let y = null;
   console.log(y);   // Output: null
   ```

6. **Symbol** (ES6+):

   o Represents a unique and immutable value, often used as identifiers for object properties.

   o Example:

   ```
   javascript
   ```

   ```
   const symbol1 = Symbol('description');
   const symbol2 = Symbol('description');
   console.log(symbol1  ===  symbol2);    //
   Output: false
   ```

These primitive data types are essential for working with variables, comparisons, and controlling the flow of data in JavaScript programs.

Declaring and Manipulating Variables

In JavaScript, variables are containers for storing data values. There are several ways to declare variables, and the way they are declared impacts their scope and reusability. JavaScript provides three keywords to declare variables: `var`, `let`, and `const`.

- **Declaring Variables with `var`:**
    - The `var` keyword is used to declare variables in older JavaScript code. Variables declared with `var` are function-scoped, meaning they are accessible throughout the function in which they are declared. However, they can cause issues with variable hoisting and block scope, which led to the introduction of `let` and `const` in ES6.

    Example:

    ```javascript
    var name = "Alice";
    console.log(name);   // Output: Alice
    ```

- **Declaring Variables with `let`:**
    - The `let` keyword is used to declare block-scoped variables, meaning the variable is only accessible within the block (e.g., inside loops or

conditionals) where it is defined. `let` was introduced in ES6 to address the limitations of `var`.

Example:

```javascript
let age = 25;
if (true) {
    let age = 30;  // Block-scoped variable
    console.log(age);  // Output: 30
}
console.log(age);  // Output: 25 (the outer age variable)
```

- **Declaring Variables with `const`:**
  - The `const` keyword is used to declare variables that should not be reassigned after their initial value is set. `const` is also block-scoped, but the difference is that the value of a `const` variable cannot be changed after assignment. This is particularly useful for creating constants or values that should remain unchanged.

Example:

```javascript
```

```
const pi = 3.14;
console.log(pi);   // Output: 3.14
// pi = 3.14159;   // Error: Assignment to constant
variable.
```

Note: While you cannot reassign a `const` variable, if the variable refers to an object or array, the contents of the object or array can still be modified.

Example:

```
javascript
```

```
const person = { name: "John", age: 30 };
person.age = 31;   // Modifying object properties
is allowed
console.log(person.age);   // Output: 31
```

Differences Between `var`*,* `let`*, and* `const` *in JavaScript*

The primary differences between `var`, `let`, and `const` lie in their **scope**, **hoisting behavior**, and **reassignability**:

Feature	var	let	const
Scope	Function-scoped	Block-scoped	Block-scoped
Hoisting	Hoisted, initialized to undefined	Hoisted, not initialized	Hoisted, not initialized

Feature	var	let	const
Reassignability	Reassignable	Reassignable	Not reassignable
Redeclaration	Can be redeclared in the same scope	Cannot be redeclared in the same scope	Cannot be redeclared in the same scope

- `var` is function-scoped and can be redeclared within the same scope, but it can lead to issues like variable hoisting (declaring variables at the top of the function scope unintentionally).
- `let` and `const` are block-scoped, meaning they are confined to the block (enclosed by curly braces) where they are declared. They also solve hoisting issues by not allowing access to variables before they are declared.

Real-World Example: Building a Dynamic Content Display on a Webpage Using JavaScript

Now that we understand how to declare variables and manipulate data types, let's create a real-world interactive feature using

JavaScript. We will build a dynamic content display on a webpage that changes based on user input.

Goal: Create a webpage that lets the user select their favorite color from a list and then displays a message with their choice.

1. HTML Structure:

html

```
<!DOCTYPE html>
<html lang="en">
<head>
    <meta charset="UTF-8">
    <meta name="viewport" content="width=device-width,
initial-scale=1.0">
    <title>Dynamic Content Display</title>
</head>
<body>
    <h1>Choose Your Favorite Color</h1>

    <!-- Dropdown list for color selection -->
    <select id="colorSelect">
        <option value="red">Red</option>
        <option value="green">Green</option>
        <option value="blue">Blue</option>
        <option value="yellow">Yellow</option>
    </select>

    <!-- Button to trigger the change -->
```

```html
    <button                onclick="displayColor()">Show
Color</button>


    <!-- Paragraph to display the result -->
    <p id="result"></p>


    <script src="script.js"></script>
</body>
</html>
```

2. JavaScript Code (script.js):

javascript

```javascript
// Function to display the selected color
function displayColor() {
    // Get the selected color value from the dropdown
    const             colorSelect             =
document.getElementById("colorSelect");
    const selectedColor = colorSelect.value;


    // Get the result element where the message will be
displayed
    const result = document.getElementById("result");


    // Change the text content and background color
based on the selected color
    result.textContent = `You selected the color:
${selectedColor}`;
    result.style.backgroundColor = selectedColor;
}
```

Explanation:

- In the HTML part, we create a dropdown (`<select>`) with different color options and a button that calls the `displayColor()` function when clicked.
- In the JavaScript code, we:
    1. Retrieve the selected value from the dropdown using `document.getElementById()` and the `.value` property.
    2. Update the content of the paragraph with the id `result` using `.textContent`.
    3. Change the background color of the result paragraph based on the selected color using the `.style.backgroundColor` property.

Output: When the user selects a color from the dropdown and clicks the "Show Color" button, the page dynamically updates to display the selected color and background.

Summary

In this chapter, we delved into JavaScript's primitive data types, explored how to declare and manipulate variables, and discussed the differences between `var`, `let`, and `const`. These concepts are fundamental in JavaScript programming, as they help manage data and control the behavior of your code. We also applied this knowledge to build a dynamic content display on a webpage, demonstrating how JavaScript can be used to create interactive and responsive web experiences. Understanding variables, data types, and how to use them effectively is essential for writing clean, maintainable, and efficient JavaScript code.

Chapter 8: Functions and Loops in JavaScript

Creating and Using Functions in JavaScript

Functions in JavaScript allow you to group code into reusable blocks. By using functions, you can avoid repetition, improve code organization, and make your code more readable and maintainable. Functions can take input (parameters), perform operations, and return output (values).

- **Defining Functions**: You define a function in JavaScript using the `function` keyword, followed by the function name, parameters in parentheses, and a block of code within curly braces `{}`.

  Syntax:

  ```javascript
  function functionName(parameters) {
      // Code to execute
  }
  ```

  - Example:

    ```javascript
    function greet(name) {
    ```

```
        console.log(`Hello, ${name}!`);
    }
    greet("Alice");   // Output: Hello, Alice!
```

- **Returning Values**: Functions can also return values using the `return` keyword. This allows the function to send a result back to the code that called it.

Example:

javascript

```
function add(a, b) {
    return a + b;
}
let result = add(5, 3);
console.log(result);   // Output: 8
```

- **Function Expressions**: JavaScript also allows you to define functions as expressions. A function expression is a function that is assigned to a variable.

Example:

javascript

```
const subtract = function(a, b) {
    return a - b;
};
console.log(subtract(10, 4));   // Output: 6
```

- **Arrow Functions (ES6+)**: Arrow functions are a shorter syntax for writing functions, especially useful for small, anonymous functions. They also handle the `this` keyword differently.

Example:

javascript

```
const multiply = (a, b) => a * b;
console.log(multiply(4, 2));   // Output: 8
```

For, While, and forEach Loops in JavaScript

Loops are essential in programming for iterating over data, performing repetitive tasks, and handling arrays or lists of items. In JavaScript, you have several types of loops at your disposal:

1. **For Loop**: The `for` loop is used to run a block of code a specific number of times. It is typically used when you know in advance how many times you want the loop to execute.

   Syntax:

   javascript

   ```
   for (let i = 0; i < 10; i++) {
       // Code to execute
   }
   ```

   o Example:

```
javascript

for (let i = 0; i < 5; i++) {
    console.log(i);  // Output: 0, 1, 2, 3,
4
}
```

2. **While Loop**: The `while` loop runs as long as a given condition is true. It is useful when you don't know exactly how many times the loop should run, but you do know the condition that needs to be satisfied.

Syntax:

```
javascript

while (condition) {
    // Code to execute
}
```

○ **Example:**

```
javascript

let i = 0;
while (i < 5) {
    console.log(i);  // Output: 0, 1, 2, 3,
4
    i++;
}
```

3. **forEach Loop**: The `forEach` method is an array method used to execute a provided function once for each element in the array. It is more concise and readable than a `for` loop when dealing with arrays.

Syntax:

```javascript
array.forEach(function(element) {
    // Code to execute for each element
});
```

- **Example**:

```javascript
const numbers = [1, 2, 3, 4, 5];
numbers.forEach(function(number) {
    console.log(number);   // Output: 1, 2, 3, 4, 5
});
```

Arrow Function Syntax: You can also use an arrow function with `forEach` for a more concise syntax.

```javascript
numbers.forEach(number => console.log(number));
// Output: 1, 2, 3, 4, 5
```

Real-World Example: Writing a JavaScript Script to Process Form Input from Users

Let's apply the knowledge of functions, loops, and data processing to build a small real-world example. In this case, we will create a form where users can input their names and ages. When the form is submitted, we'll use JavaScript to validate the input and display the users' data in a dynamic list.

1. **HTML Form**:

```html
html
```

```html
<!DOCTYPE html>
<html lang="en">
<head>
    <meta charset="UTF-8">
    <meta name="viewport" content="width=device-width, initial-scale=1.0">
    <title>User Data Form</title>
</head>
<body>
    <h1>User Information</h1>
    <form id="userForm">
        <label for="name">Name:</label>
        <input type="text" id="name" required>
        <br>
        <label for="age">Age:</label>
        <input type="number" id="age" required>
        <br>
```

```html
        <button type="submit">Submit</button>
    </form>

    <h2>Submitted Data</h2>
    <ul id="userList"></ul>

    <script src="script.js"></script>
</body>
</html>
```

2. **JavaScript to Process Form Input (script.js):**

javascript

```javascript
// Get the form element and the user list
const                    form                    =
document.getElementById("userForm");
const                  userList                   =
document.getElementById("userList");

// Function to handle form submission
form.addEventListener("submit",   function(event)
{
    event.preventDefault();  // Prevent form from
submitting the default way

    // Get the values from the input fields
    const                   name                   =
document.getElementById("name").value;
    const                   age                    =
document.getElementById("age").value;
```

```
// Validate the input values
if (name === "" || age === "") {
    alert("Please fill in both fields.");
    return;
}

// Create a new list item to display the
user's data
const                    listItem              =
document.createElement("li");
listItem.textContent = `Name: ${name}, Age:
${age}`;

// Append the new list item to the user list
userList.appendChild(listItem);

// Clear the form fields
form.reset();
});
```

Explanation:

- The HTML form allows users to input their name and age and submit the form.
- In the JavaScript file:
  - We use `addEventListener()` to capture the form submission event and prevent the default behavior using `event.preventDefault()`.

- o We retrieve the values from the input fields using `document.getElementById()`.
- o We check that both fields are filled in. If not, we display an alert and stop further processing.
- o If the inputs are valid, we create a new list item (`<li>`) to display the user's name and age in the `userList` unordered list.
- o After appending the new data to the list, we reset the form inputs.

Output:

- After submitting the form with valid data, the user's name and age will be displayed in a list below the form.

Best Practices for Managing Scope and Closures in JavaScript

As you work with JavaScript, managing scope and understanding closures are crucial for writing clean, efficient, and bug-free code.

1. **Scope Management**:
   - o **Global Scope**: Variables declared outside of any functions are in the global scope, meaning they can be accessed anywhere in the code.
   - o **Function Scope**: Variables declared inside a function are local to that function and cannot be accessed from outside.

- o **Block Scope**: Variables declared with `let` and `const` are block-scoped, meaning they are only accessible within the block they were defined in (e.g., inside loops or conditionals).

Best Practice:

- o Always prefer block-scoped variables (`let`, `const`) over function-scoped variables (`var`) to avoid unwanted side effects and confusion in your code.
- o Limit the use of global variables to avoid conflicts and maintain encapsulation.

2. **Closures**: A **closure** is a function that retains access to the variables from its outer (enclosing) function, even after the outer function has finished executing. Closures are powerful and can be used for data encapsulation and creating private variables.

Example of Closure:

javascript

```
function outerFunction() {
    let count = 0;

    return function innerFunction() {
```

```
            count++;
            console.log(count);
        };
    }
```

```
const increment = outerFunction();   // Create a
closure
increment();   // Output: 1
increment();   // Output: 2
```

In this example:

- o `innerFunction` is a closure because it retains access to the `count` variable from the `outerFunction` even after `outerFunction` has finished executing.
- o Each time `increment()` is called, it increases the `count` variable.

3. **Avoiding Common Mistakes**:

- o Avoid excessive nesting of functions or closures, which can make your code harder to read and maintain.
- o Be mindful of variable shadowing, where a variable in an inner scope has the same name as one in an outer scope. This can lead to confusion and unexpected behavior.

Summary

In this chapter, we explored how to create and use functions in JavaScript, as well as the various types of loops available: `for`, `while`, and `forEach`. We also implemented a real-world example of processing user input from a form and displaying dynamic content. Finally, we discussed best practices for managing variable scope and closures, which are essential concepts for writing clean, efficient, and maintainable JavaScript code. By mastering these techniques, you'll be able to write more robust, interactive web applications and handle data processing more effectively.

Chapter 9: Introduction to C++

The Role of C++ in System Programming and Performance-Critical Applications

C++ is a powerful, high-performance programming language that has been a cornerstone of system-level programming and software development for decades. It is widely used in performance-critical applications where both efficiency and fine control over hardware resources are essential. Some key areas where C++ excels include:

1. **System Programming**:
   - C++ is frequently used to develop system software, such as operating systems, device drivers, and embedded systems. This is because C++ provides low-level access to memory and system resources while maintaining high-level programming capabilities. It allows developers to write code that is both close to the hardware and highly efficient, making it ideal for operating system kernels and real-time systems.
2. **Performance-Critical Applications**:
   - C++ is well-known for its performance due to its ability to directly manipulate hardware and memory. Many applications that require high

performance, such as video games, simulations, financial modeling, and high-frequency trading systems, are written in C++ to achieve the necessary speed and efficiency.

- o C++ allows developers to use advanced features like pointers, manual memory management, and multithreading to optimize the performance of their applications.

3. **Game Development**:
   - o C++ has long been the language of choice for developing high-performance video games. Game engines like Unreal Engine are written in C++, and the language is used to build both 2D and 3D games. Its performance is crucial in rendering graphics and simulating complex game environments.

4. **Real-Time Systems**:
   - o C++ is commonly used in applications that require real-time processing, such as automotive systems, medical devices, and industrial control systems. The ability to directly manage memory and optimize resource usage is a significant advantage in such domains.

5. **Software Libraries**:

o C++ is also heavily used to develop software libraries, especially those that provide low-level operations or high-performance algorithms. Libraries like Boost and STL (Standard Template Library) provide optimized and reusable components for C++ programs, further increasing the efficiency and productivity of developers.

Setting Up a C++ Development Environment

To start programming in C++, you need to set up a development environment that includes a text editor (or IDE) and a C++ compiler. Here's how to get started:

1. **Installing a C++ Compiler**:
   o C++ programs need to be compiled before they can be run. A C++ compiler translates your C++ code into machine code that the computer can understand.
   o On **Windows**, you can install **MinGW** (Minimalist GNU for Windows) or use Microsoft's **Visual Studio**.
   o On **Mac OS X**, you can install **Xcode**, which comes with a C++ compiler.

- On **Linux**, you can install **GCC** (GNU Compiler Collection) via the terminal by running `sudo apt-get install g++`.

2. **Choosing an IDE or Text Editor**:

   - While you can use any text editor to write C++ code, an Integrated Development Environment (IDE) can make the process easier by providing syntax highlighting, debugging tools, and auto-completion.

   - Some popular IDEs for C++ include:

     - **Visual Studio**: A powerful IDE for Windows users, with robust debugging tools and excellent C++ support.

     - **Code::Blocks**: An open-source, cross-platform IDE for C++ development.

     - **CLion**: A cross-platform IDE by JetBrains that is popular for C++ development.

   - Alternatively, lightweight text editors like **Visual Studio Code** or **Sublime Text** can be used, with C++ extensions installed.

3. **Compiling and Running C++ Code**:

   - After installing a compiler and text editor, you can write your first C++ program and compile it. For example:

```cpp

#include <iostream>

int main() {
    std::cout << "Hello, World!" << std::endl;
    return 0;
}
```

o   Save this as `hello.cpp`, then compile and run it using the following commands:

- **On Linux/Mac OS**:

```bash

g++ hello.cpp -o hello
./hello
```

- **On Windows (MinGW)**:

```bash

g++ hello.cpp -o hello.exe
hello.exe
```

4. This will output:
5.
6. Hello, World!

Writing Your First C++ Program and Understanding Its Structure

A basic C++ program follows a simple structure:

1. **Preprocessor Directives**:
   - C++ uses `#include` to include libraries or header files at the beginning of the program. The most common library used in the initial programs is `<iostream>`, which allows input and output operations.

cpp

```cpp
#include <iostream>
```

2. **Main Function**:
   - The `main()` function is the entry point of every C++ program. The program starts executing from here.

cpp

```cpp
int main() {
    // Code goes here
    return 0;  // Indicates successful execution
}
```

3. **Output to Console**:

- o The `std::cout` object is used to display output in the console. The `<<` operator is used to send data to `std::cout`.

cpp

```
std::cout << "Hello, World!" << std::endl;
```

4. **Returning from `main()`:**

- o `main()` must return an integer value. A return value of `0` typically indicates that the program executed successfully.

cpp

```
return 0;
```

Here's a simple example that demonstrates the structure of a C++ program:

cpp

```
#include <iostream>   // Include the iostream library
for input/output

int main() {
    std::cout << "Welcome to C++ programming!" <<
std::endl;   // Print message
    return 0;   // Exit the program
}
```

Real-World Example: A Simple Text-Based Game in C++

Let's now apply our knowledge of C++ syntax and structure to create a simple text-based guessing game. In this game, the user must guess a randomly generated number between 1 and 100.

1. **Game Concept**:
   - The program will generate a random number between 1 and 100.
   - The player will be prompted to guess the number.
   - The program will tell the player whether the guess is too high, too low, or correct.
   - The player will keep guessing until they get the correct answer.

2. **Code Implementation**:

cpp

```cpp
#include <iostream>   // For input and output
#include <cstdlib>    // For generating random numbers
#include <ctime>      // For seeding the random number
generator

int main() {
    // Seed the random number generator with the
current time
    std::srand(std::time(0));
```

```cpp
    int randomNumber = std::rand() % 100 + 1;    //
Generate a random number between 1 and 100

    int guess = 0;
    int attempts = 0;

    std::cout << "Welcome to the Guessing Game!" <<
std::endl;
    std::cout << "Guess the number between 1 and 100."
<< std::endl;

    // Game loop
    while (guess != randomNumber) {
        std::cout << "Enter your guess: ";
        std::cin >> guess;   // Read the player's guess
        attempts++;

        if (guess < randomNumber) {
            std::cout << "Too low! Try again." <<
std::endl;
        } else if (guess > randomNumber) {
            std::cout << "Too high! Try again." <<
std::endl;
        } else {
            std::cout << "Congratulations! You guessed
the correct number in " << attempts << " attempts!" <<
std::endl;
        }
    }

    return 0;   // Exit the program
```

```
}
```

Explanation:

- We use `std::rand()` to generate a random number, and `std::time(0)` is used to seed the random number generator to ensure the numbers are different each time the program runs.
- We use a `while` loop to repeatedly ask the user for a guess until they guess the correct number.
- The `std::cin` function is used to accept input from the user.
- After each guess, the program will print whether the guess was too high, too low, or correct.

Example Output:

```mathematica
Welcome to the Guessing Game!
Guess the number between 1 and 100.
Enter your guess: 50
Too low! Try again.
Enter your guess: 75
Too high! Try again.
Enter your guess: 62
Too low! Try again.
Enter your guess: 68
```

```
Congratulations! You guessed the correct number in 4
attempts!
```

Summary

In this chapter, we introduced C++ and its role in system programming and performance-critical applications. We explored how to set up a development environment and write your first C++ program, learning about the basic structure of a C++ program. We then applied this knowledge to create a simple text-based guessing game, demonstrating how to use control flow, input/output, and random number generation in C++. By mastering these fundamental concepts, you'll be able to create more complex and efficient C++ programs for various applications.

Chapter 10: Data Structures and Algorithms in C++

Common Data Structures in C++: Arrays, Lists, and Hash Tables

Data structures are fundamental to efficiently storing, accessing, and managing data in software applications. In C++, several built-in data structures are commonly used, each with unique advantages depending on the problem you're trying to solve. Let's discuss three common data structures: **arrays**, **lists**, and **hash tables**.

1. **Arrays**:
   - An array is a collection of elements of the same type stored in contiguous memory locations. In C++, arrays are fixed in size, meaning the size must be defined at the time of creation.
   - Arrays are ideal for situations where you need fast, constant-time access to elements via their index.

   Example:

   cpp

   ```
   int numbers[5] = {1, 2, 3, 4, 5};
   std::cout << numbers[2];  // Output: 3
   ```

- o In the example above, `numbers` is an array that holds 5 integers. You can access individual elements using an index, with indices starting from 0.

2. **Lists**:

- o In C++, the `std::list` is a doubly linked list that allows for efficient insertion and deletion of elements at both ends (front and back), but accessing elements by index is slower than arrays.

- o Lists are ideal when you need to frequently add or remove elements, especially from the beginning or middle of the collection.

Example:

cpp

```cpp
#include <iostream>
#include <list>

int main() {
    std::list<int> numbers = {1, 2, 3, 4, 5};
    numbers.push_back(6);   // Add 6 to the end
    numbers.push_front(0); // Add 0 to the front

    for (int num : numbers) {
```

```
        std::cout << num << " ";  // Output: 0 1
    2 3 4 5 6
        }
    }
```

- o The `std::list` allows you to efficiently insert and remove elements from any position, but you can't access elements directly by index without iterating through the list.

3. **Hash Tables**:

   - o A hash table (or hash map) is a data structure that stores key-value pairs and uses a hash function to compute an index (hash) into an array of buckets or slots, from which the desired value can be found. In C++, the `std::unordered_map` is the most commonly used implementation of hash tables.

   - o Hash tables provide fast average time complexity for lookups, insertions, and deletions, making them ideal for situations where you need quick access to values using unique keys.

   Example:

   cpp

```cpp
#include <iostream>
#include <unordered_map>

int main() {
    std::unordered_map<std::string, int> scores;
    scores["Alice"] = 95;
    scores["Bob"] = 85;
    scores["Charlie"] = 92;

    std::cout << "Alice's score: " << scores["Alice"] << std::endl;  // Output: 95
}
```

- o The `unordered_map` allows you to store and retrieve values using a unique key. The hash function computes the location of each key-value pair in the table, ensuring fast lookups.

Understanding Algorithms and Their Time Complexity

Algorithms are step-by-step procedures or formulas for solving problems. An important aspect of algorithms is their **time complexity**, which measures the amount of time an algorithm takes to complete as a function of the size of its input. The goal is to optimize algorithms to handle large inputs efficiently.

1. **Big O Notation**:
   - o Big O notation is used to describe the upper bound of an algorithm's time complexity,

indicating the worst-case scenario for how the runtime increases as the input size grows.

- Common time complexities:
  - **O(1)**: Constant time – The runtime is independent of the input size.
  - **O(log n)**: Logarithmic time – The runtime grows logarithmically with the input size, often seen in binary search.
  - **O(n)**: Linear time – The runtime grows linearly with the input size, seen in simple loops.
  - **O(n log n)**: Linearithmic time – Often seen in efficient sorting algorithms, like mergesort and heapsort.
  - **O(n²)**: Quadratic time – Seen in algorithms with nested loops, such as bubble sort.

2. **Time Complexity Examples**:
   - **Example of O(1)**: Accessing an element in an array using an index.

cpp

```
int arr[10];
arr[5] = 100;  // Constant time operation, O(1)
```

- o **Example of O(n)**: Iterating through an array or list.

cpp

```cpp
for (int i = 0; i < 10; i++) {
    std::cout << arr[i] << std::endl;    // Linear
time, O(n)
}
```

- o **Example of O(n²)**: A nested loop that iterates over the array twice (for bubble sort or selection sort).

cpp

```cpp
for (int i = 0; i < n; i++) {
    for (int j = 0; j < n; j++) {
        // O(n²) time complexity
    }
}
```

Understanding the time complexity of different algorithms helps in choosing the right one based on the size of the input and the performance requirements of your application.

Real-World Example: Implementing a Sorting Algorithm in C++
One of the most common algorithms in computer science is **sorting**. Sorting allows you to arrange data in a specific order, often to optimize other algorithms (such as searching). Let's implement a

simple sorting algorithm called **Bubble Sort**, which repeatedly steps through the list, compares adjacent elements, and swaps them if they are in the wrong order.

1. **Bubble Sort Implementation**:
    - The Bubble Sort algorithm is easy to understand but inefficient for large datasets due to its $O(n^2)$ time complexity.

cpp

```cpp
#include <iostream>

void bubbleSort(int arr[], int n) {
    // Outer loop for each pass through the array
    for (int i = 0; i < n - 1; i++) {
        // Inner loop for comparing adjacent elements
        for (int j = 0; j < n - 1 - i; j++) {
            if (arr[j] > arr[j + 1]) {
                // Swap the elements if they are in the
wrong order
                int temp = arr[j];
                arr[j] = arr[j + 1];
                arr[j + 1] = temp;
            }
        }
    }
}
```

```cpp
int main() {
    int arr[] = {64, 34, 25, 12, 22, 11, 90};
    int n = sizeof(arr) / sizeof(arr[0]);

    std::cout << "Original array: ";
    for (int i = 0; i < n; i++) {
        std::cout << arr[i] << " ";
    }
    std::cout << std::endl;

    bubbleSort(arr, n);

    std::cout << "Sorted array: ";
    for (int i = 0; i < n; i++) {
        std::cout << arr[i] << " ";
    }
    std::cout << std::endl;

    return 0;
}
```

Explanation:

- The `bubbleSort` function repeatedly passes through the array and compares adjacent elements, swapping them if they are out of order. After each pass, the largest unsorted element "bubbles" to its correct position.
- The time complexity of Bubble Sort is $O(n^2)$ because of the nested loops.

Example Output:

```c

```

```
Original array: 64 34 25 12 22 11 90
Sorted array: 11 12 22 25 34 64 90
```

This example demonstrates a simple but inefficient sorting algorithm. For large datasets, more efficient sorting algorithms like **QuickSort** or **MergeSort** (with time complexity O(n log n)) would be preferable.

Practical Tips for Optimizing C++ Code for Performance

1. **Avoid Unnecessary Memory Allocation**:
   - Dynamic memory allocation (using `new` or `malloc`) can be expensive. If possible, use stack-based memory (local variables) or pre-allocate memory in advance for arrays and other data structures.
2. **Use Efficient Data Structures**:
   - Choose the right data structure based on the problem at hand. For example, using a **hash table** (unordered_map in C++) for fast lookups, or a **vector** (dynamic array) instead of a list when you need to access elements by index efficiently.
3. **Minimize Expensive Operations**:

- Avoid unnecessary recalculations in loops. Cache results of expensive operations or use efficient algorithms like memoization or dynamic programming when applicable.

4. **Optimize Loops**:
   - Loops are often the source of performance bottlenecks. Ensure that loops only run as many times as necessary, and consider using more efficient loop structures (e.g., avoid nested loops when possible).

5. **Use Compiler Optimizations**:
   - Modern compilers can optimize C++ code for better performance. Use optimization flags (`-O2`, `-O3` in GCC) to enable automatic performance improvements during compilation.

6. **Profile Your Code**:
   - Use profiling tools (such as `gprof`, `valgrind`, or built-in performance analyzers) to identify performance bottlenecks in your application. Focus your optimization efforts on the parts of your code that matter most.

7. **Use Smart Pointers**:
   - In C++, using raw pointers can sometimes lead to memory leaks or inefficient memory

management. Smart pointers (`std::unique_ptr,` `std::shared_ptr`) automatically handle memory management and can improve the performance of memory-heavy applications.

Summary

In this chapter, we explored common data structures in C++—arrays, lists, and hash tables—each with its own strengths and applications. We then delved into the importance of understanding algorithms and their time complexity, using sorting as an example. Finally, we discussed practical tips for optimizing C++ code for performance, including using efficient data structures, minimizing memory allocation, and leveraging compiler optimizations. By mastering data structures and algorithms, you can write more efficient and scalable C++ applications, especially when working with large datasets or performance-critical tasks.

Chapter 11: Object-Oriented Programming in C++

Understanding Classes, Objects, and Methods in C++

Object-Oriented Programming (OOP) is a fundamental programming paradigm that helps organize and structure code using the concepts of classes, objects, inheritance, polymorphism, and encapsulation. C++ is a powerful language that supports OOP, allowing developers to write modular, reusable, and maintainable code.

1. **Classes**:
   - A **class** in C++ is a blueprint for creating objects. It defines the properties (attributes) and behaviors (methods) that the objects created from the class will have.
   - A class is defined using the `class` keyword, followed by the class name and a set of curly braces `{}` to contain its members.

   Example:

   ```cpp
   class Car {
   public:
   ```

```cpp
    // Attributes (data members)
    std::string make;
    std::string model;
    int year;

    // Method (function member)
    void start() {
        std::cout << "The " << make << " " <<
model << " is starting." << std::endl;
    }
};
```

2. **Objects**:

   o An **object** is an instance of a class. Once a class is defined, you can create objects based on it. Each object can hold different values for the class's attributes and call its methods.

Example:

cpp

```cpp
int main() {
    // Creating an object of class Car
    Car myCar;
    myCar.make = "Toyota";
    myCar.model = "Corolla";
    myCar.year = 2022;
```

123

```
    myCar.start();  // Output: The Toyota Corolla
is starting.
}
```

3. **Methods**:

   o Methods are functions defined within a class that describe the behaviors of an object. Methods can manipulate the object's attributes and perform actions using them. They are often defined as public, meaning they can be accessed outside the class.

   o Methods that are part of a class and operate on the class's data members are called **member functions**.

   Example:

   cpp

```cpp
class Circle {
public:
    float radius;

    // Method to calculate the area
    float getArea() {
        return 3.14 * radius * radius;
    }
};
```

Memory Management and the Importance of Pointers in C++

Memory management is a critical aspect of C++ programming because it provides the programmer with fine-grained control over memory allocation and deallocation. Unlike languages like Python or Java, where memory management is handled automatically, C++ requires the programmer to explicitly manage memory. Pointers and dynamic memory allocation are central to this process.

1. **Pointers**:
    - A **pointer** is a variable that stores the memory address of another variable. Pointers are powerful tools that allow for efficient memory management and enable dynamic memory allocation.
    - The declaration of a pointer uses the * symbol.

   Example:

   cpp

   ```
   int num = 10;
   int* ptr = &num;  // ptr stores the memory address
   of num
   std::cout << *ptr;  // Output: 10 (dereferencing
   the pointer)
   ```

2. **Dynamic Memory Allocation**:

- C++ allows dynamic memory allocation using the `new` and `delete` operators. The `new` operator allocates memory for a variable or object on the heap, and the `delete` operator deallocates the memory.

Example:

cpp

```
int* ptr = new int;  // Allocates memory for an
integer
*ptr = 25;  // Assign value to the allocated
memory
std::cout << *ptr;  // Output: 25
delete ptr;  // Deallocates memory
```

3. **Using Pointers in Classes**:
   - Pointers are especially useful in object-oriented programming when dealing with dynamic memory allocation and when creating objects dynamically using `new`.
   - For example, a pointer can be used to create objects on the heap, which allows objects to persist even after the scope of the function ends.

Example:

```cpp
cpp

class Car {
public:
    std::string make;
    std::string model;

    void start() {
        std::cout << "Starting the " << make <<
" " << model << std::endl;
    }
};

int main() {
    Car* carPtr = new Car;   // Dynamically
allocate memory for a Car object
    carPtr->make = "Tesla";
    carPtr->model = "Model 3";

    carPtr->start();   // Output: Starting the
Tesla Model 3

    delete carPtr;  // Deallocate memory
}
```

Real-World Example: Building a Bank Account System in C++
Now, let's build a simple bank account system in C++ that allows users to deposit and withdraw money, check their balance, and display account information. We'll use classes, methods, and pointers to manage the system.

1. **Define the `BankAccount` Class:**

   o **The `BankAccount` class will have attributes like** `accountNumber`, `balance`, **and methods like** `deposit()`, `withdraw()`, **and** `displayInfo()`.

cpp

```cpp
#include <iostream>
#include <string>

class BankAccount {
private:
    std::string accountHolder;
    double balance;

public:
    // Constructor to initialize the account with
holder's name and initial balance
    BankAccount(std::string       holder,       double
initialBalance) {
        accountHolder = holder;
        balance = initialBalance;
    }

    // Method to deposit money into the account
    void deposit(double amount) {
        if (amount > 0) {
            balance += amount;
            std::cout << "$" << amount << " deposited.
New balance: $" << balance << std::endl;
```

```cpp
        } else {
            std::cout << "Invalid deposit amount!" <<
std::endl;
        }
    }


    // Method to withdraw money from the account
    void withdraw(double amount) {
        if (amount > 0 && amount <= balance) {
            balance -= amount;
            std::cout << "$" << amount << " withdrawn.
New balance: $" << balance << std::endl;
        } else {
            std::cout << "Insufficient funds or invalid
withdrawal amount!" << std::endl;
        }
    }


    // Method to display account information
    void displayInfo() {
        std::cout   <<   "Account   Holder:   "   <<
accountHolder << std::endl;
        std::cout  <<  "Balance:  $"  <<  balance  <<
std::endl;
    }
};

int main() {
    // Creating a BankAccount object dynamically using
a pointer
```

```
    BankAccount*  myAccount  =  new  BankAccount("John
Doe", 500.0);

    myAccount->deposit(200.0);   // Deposit $200
    myAccount->withdraw(50.0);   // Withdraw $50
    myAccount->displayInfo();      // Display account
details

    delete myAccount;  // Deallocate memory
    return 0;
}
```

Explanation:

- The `BankAccount` class has two private attributes: `accountHolder` and `balance`. It also has three public methods: `deposit()`, `withdraw()`, and `displayInfo()`.
- The `deposit()` method adds money to the balance, while the `withdraw()` method subtracts money from the balance (if sufficient funds are available).
- The `displayInfo()` method outputs the account holder's name and the current balance.
- In the `main()` function, we dynamically create a `BankAccount` object using the `new` keyword and interact with it using the methods defined in the class.
- After we are done with the object, we use `delete` to free the allocated memory.

Example Output:

```bash
$200 deposited. New balance: $700
$50 withdrawn. New balance: $650
Account Holder: John Doe
Balance: $650
```

Best Practices for Using Classes and Avoiding Common Pitfalls in C++

1. **Encapsulation:**
   - Always encapsulate data members by making them private and providing getter and setter methods to access and modify them. This ensures that data is protected and can only be manipulated through controlled methods.

   Example:

```cpp
class BankAccount {
private:
    double balance;

public:
    double getBalance() const { return balance;
}
```

CODE CRAFTING: THE COMPLETE GUIDE TO MODERN PROGRAMMING LANGUAGES

```
        void  setBalance(double  amount)  {  balance  =
    amount;  }
    };
```

2. **Use Constructors for Initialization**:
   - o Use constructors to initialize your objects, ensuring that they are properly set up when created. This avoids uninitialized variables and ensures consistency in your objects.

3. **Avoid Memory Leaks**:
   - o Always free dynamically allocated memory using `delete` to prevent memory leaks. When using pointers, ensure that each `new` operation has a corresponding `delete` operation.

4. **Use Smart Pointers**:
   - o For better memory management, consider using smart pointers (`std::unique_ptr`, `std::shared_ptr`) in modern C++ to automatically manage memory and prevent memory leaks.

5. **Avoid Excessive Use of Global Variables**:
   - o Global variables should be avoided as much as possible because they can create dependencies that make the code harder to maintain and debug.

6. **Be Mindful of Object Slicing**:
   - When working with inheritance, avoid object slicing, which occurs when an object of a derived class is assigned to a base class object, causing the derived class data to be "sliced" off.

Solution: Use pointers or references to the base class instead of objects.

cpp

```
Base* basePtr = new Derived();
```

7. **Implement Constructors and Assignment Operators**:
   - If your class involves dynamic memory allocation or contains pointers, you should implement a **constructor** and an **assignment operator** to manage deep copies of objects.

Example:

cpp

```
class BankAccount {
private:
    double* balance;
public:
    // constructor
    BankAccount(const BankAccount& other) {
```

```
        balance = new double(*other.balance);
    }
};
```

Summary

In this chapter, we explored the concepts of object-oriented programming in C++, focusing on classes, objects, and methods. We learned how to manage memory using pointers and dynamic allocation, and we created a real-world example of a bank account system. By following best practices such as encapsulation, using constructors for initialization, and managing memory carefully, you can write clean, efficient, and maintainable C++ code. Mastering these concepts will help you write robust applications that can handle complex data and perform optimally in a variety of scenarios.

Chapter 12: Modern Features in C++:

Smart Pointers, Lambda Functions, and More

Introduction to Advanced Features in Modern C++

C++ is a language that continuously evolves, and the introduction of newer versions has brought a wealth of advanced features that make coding more efficient, safer, and easier to manage. Some of these modern features, introduced primarily in C++11, C++14, C++17, and C++20, significantly enhance the language's capabilities. Key modern features in C++ include:

- **Smart Pointers**: These manage dynamic memory and prevent memory leaks.
- **Lambda Functions**: Anonymous functions that can be defined inline, making code more concise and readable.
- **Range-based Loops**: A more convenient and safer way to iterate over collections.
- **Move Semantics**: A mechanism for optimizing the transfer of resources between objects.
- **Type Inference**: Using `auto` for automatic type deduction, reducing boilerplate code.

These features allow developers to write more readable, maintainable, and efficient code, making C++ programming even more powerful. This chapter will focus on three important features:

smart pointers, lambda functions, and efficient data processing using these features.

How Smart Pointers Help Manage Memory in C++

In traditional C++ programming, managing dynamic memory with `new` and `delete` can be error-prone and lead to memory leaks or dangling pointers. To help mitigate these issues, **smart pointers** were introduced in C++11 as part of the Standard Library. Smart pointers automatically manage memory by ensuring that memory is freed when it is no longer needed, and they handle resource management automatically.

There are three types of smart pointers in C++:

1. `std::unique_ptr`:
   - **Ownership**: A `unique_ptr` represents exclusive ownership of an object. There can be only one `unique_ptr` to a given resource at a time, and it automatically destroys the object when it goes out of scope.
   - **Use case**: Use `unique_ptr` when you need a single owner of the object.
   - **Example**:

   ```cpp
   cpp

   #include <iostream>
   ```

```
#include <memory>

class Dog {
public:
    void bark() { std::cout << "Woof!" <<
std::endl; }
};

int main() {
    std::unique_ptr<Dog>        dogPtr       =
std::make_unique<Dog>();
    dogPtr->bark();  // Output: Woof!
}
```

- o The memory occupied by the `Dog` object will be automatically deallocated when `dogPtr` goes out of scope.

2. `std::shared_ptr`:

  - o **Shared Ownership**: A `shared_ptr` allows multiple pointers to share ownership of the same resource. The resource is deleted only when the last `shared_ptr` pointing to it is destroyed.

  - o **Use case**: Use `shared_ptr` when multiple parts of the program need to share ownership of an object.

  - o **Example**:

cpp

```cpp
#include <iostream>
#include <memory>

class Dog {
public:
    void bark() { std::cout << "Woof!" <<
std::endl; }
};

int main() {
    std::shared_ptr<Dog>        dogPtr1        =
std::make_shared<Dog>();
    std::shared_ptr<Dog>        dogPtr2        =
dogPtr1;  // Both pointers share ownership
    dogPtr1->bark();  // Output: Woof!
    dogPtr2->bark();  // Output: Woof!
}
```

o **Both** dogPtr1 **and** dogPtr2 **point to the same** Dog **object, and the object is deallocated once the last** shared_ptr **is destroyed.**

3. `std::weak_ptr`:

   o **Non-owning Pointer**: A weak_ptr is a non-owning reference to an object managed by shared_ptr. It prevents the object from being kept alive solely due to references from `weak_ptr` and helps avoid circular references.

- o **Use case**: Use `weak_ptr` to observe objects managed by `shared_ptr` without affecting their lifetime.
- o **Example**:

cpp

```cpp
#include <iostream>
#include <memory>

class Dog {
public:
    void bark() { std::cout << "Woof!" <<
std::endl; }
};

int main() {
    std::shared_ptr<Dog>       dogPtr      =
std::make_shared<Dog>();
    std::weak_ptr<Dog>       weakDogPtr    =
dogPtr;  // Observes dogPtr without owning
it

    if       (auto       sharedPtr       =
weakDogPtr.lock()) {
        sharedPtr->bark();    // Output:
Woof!
```

```
        } else {
            std::cout << "The dog is no longer
available!" << std::endl;
        }
    }
```

Understanding Lambda Functions and Their Uses

Lambda functions were introduced in C++11 and provide a powerful and concise way to define anonymous functions directly in the body of other functions. They are particularly useful for short-lived functions or functions used as arguments to other functions (such as sorting or filtering operations).

1. **Basic Syntax of a Lambda Function**: The syntax for a lambda function is as follows:

   cpp

   ```
   [captures] (parameters) -> return_type { body }
   ```

   o **captures**: A list of variables from the surrounding scope that the lambda can access. This is often used when the lambda needs to use external variables.

   o **parameters**: The parameters that the lambda function will take.

   o **return_type**: The return type of the lambda function (optional; inferred automatically).

- body: The block of code that constitutes the function's body.

2. **Example of a Simple Lambda Function**:

cpp

```
#include <iostream>
#include <vector>
#include <algorithm>

int main() {
    std::vector<int> numbers = {1, 2, 3, 4, 5};

    // Lambda that prints each number
    std::for_each(numbers.begin(),
numbers.end(), [](int num) {
        std::cout << num << " ";
    });
    std::cout << std::endl;   // Output: 1 2 3 4
5
}
```

3. **Lambda with Captures**: Lambdas can capture variables from the surrounding scope by reference or by value. The syntax for capturing is as follows:

   - [&]: Capture by reference (default capture by reference for all variables).
   - [=]: Capture by value (default capture by value for all variables).

o   [x, &y]: Capture x by value and y by reference.

Example:

cpp

```cpp
int main() {
    int a = 10, b = 20;

    auto add = [a, &b]() {
        return a + b;   // 'a' captured by value,
'b' captured by reference
    };

    b = 30;   // Modify b after lambda definition
    std::cout << add() << std::endl;   // Output:
40 (a + b = 10 + 30)
}
```

4. **Using Lambdas with Standard Library Algorithms**: One of the most common uses of lambdas is in combination with C++'s powerful standard library algorithms (like std::sort, std::find_if, etc.).

Example:

cpp

```cpp
#include <iostream>
#include <vector>
```

```cpp
#include <algorithm>

int main() {
    std::vector<int> numbers = {5, 3, 8, 1, 4};

    // Sort the vector in descending order using
a lambda
    std::sort(numbers.begin(),    numbers.end(),
[](int a, int b) {
        return a > b;  // Sort in descending order
    });

    for (int num : numbers) {
        std::cout << num << " ";
    }
    std::cout << std::endl;   // Output: 8 5 4 3
1
}
```

Real-World Example: Implementing an Efficient Data Processing System in C++

In this example, we will implement a simple data processing system that processes a list of integers. The system will filter out negative numbers, sort the remaining numbers, and then perform a transformation (doubling each value). We'll use modern C++ features, including smart pointers and lambda functions, to handle the data efficiently.

cpp

```cpp
#include <iostream>
#include <vector>
#include <memory>
#include <algorithm>

int main() {
    // Creating a vector using a smart pointer
    std::unique_ptr<std::vector<int>>      data      =
std::make_unique<std::vector<int>>({10, -5, 3, -1, 8,
-7, 4});

    // Step 1: Remove negative numbers using a lambda
function with erase-remove idiom
    data->erase(std::remove_if(data->begin(),    data-
>end(), [](int n) { return n < 0; }), data->end());

    // Step 2: Sort the remaining numbers in ascending
order
    std::sort(data->begin(), data->end());

    // Step 3: Double each number using a lambda
function
    std::transform(data->begin(),  data->end(),  data-
>begin(), [](int n) { return n * 2; });

    // Step 4: Print the final processed data
    std::cout << "Processed data: ";
    for (int n : *data) {
        std::cout << n << " ";
    }
    std::cout << std::endl;  // Output: 6 8 10 16 20
```

}

Explanation:

- We use a **smart pointer** (`std::unique_ptr`) to manage the dynamic memory of the vector. This ensures that memory is automatically cleaned up when the pointer goes out of scope.
- **Lambda functions** are used to:
  - Remove negative numbers from the vector using `std::remove_if`.
  - Sort the vector in ascending order using `std::sort`.
  - Double the values of the vector using `std::transform`.
- The code is concise and efficient, with no manual memory management required thanks to smart pointers.

Summary

In this chapter, we explored several advanced features in modern C++, including **smart pointers** and **lambda functions**. We learned how smart pointers help automate memory management and prevent common memory-related issues. Lambda functions were introduced as a powerful tool for writing concise, inline functions, especially in combination with standard library algorithms. Finally, we implemented a real-world data processing system that showcases these modern C++ features. By using these tools effectively, you can write safer, more efficient, and cleaner C++ code that leverages the full power of the language.

Chapter 13: Web Development with Python: Flask and Django

Introduction to Web Development Frameworks: Flask vs Django

Web development frameworks provide developers with tools and libraries to simplify the process of building web applications. Python has two popular web development frameworks: **Flask** and **Django**. Both are highly capable but have different philosophies and use cases. Let's break down each framework and how they are used in Python web development.

1. **Flask**:

   o **Flask** is a lightweight, micro web framework designed to be simple and easy to use. Flask does not come with many built-in features, making it an excellent choice for developers who want to build small or custom applications without unnecessary overhead.

   o **Flexibility**: Flask is minimalistic, giving developers more control over the components they want to use. It allows you to choose your tools, such as the database, form handling, and authentication, as opposed to providing an all-in-one solution.

- o **When to Use**: Flask is ideal for small to medium-sized projects, prototypes, or applications where you need fine-grained control over the web stack.

2. **Django**:
   - o **Django** is a full-stack web framework that comes with a lot of built-in features, including authentication, an admin panel, database migrations, and form handling. Django follows the "batteries-included" philosophy, which means it provides most of the tools developers need to build robust web applications.
   - o **Convention over Configuration**: Django emphasizes the use of pre-built conventions, making it easier for developers to build scalable applications quickly without having to make too many decisions on the configuration.
   - o **When to Use**: Django is suited for larger projects where you need to rapidly develop complex web applications, such as e-commerce sites, social networks, or content management systems (CMS).

Comparison Table: Flask vs Django

Feature	Flask	Django
Philosophy	Micro-framework, minimalistic	Full-stack framework, batteries-included
Learning Curve	Easier, more flexible	Steeper, but well-documented
Customization	High, allows full control	Less flexible, but comes with built-in tools
Built-in Features	Very few; developers add tools as needed	Rich set of built-in features (admin panel, authentication)
Use Case	Small to medium apps, quick prototypes	Large-scale, complex web apps

Setting Up a Web Server with Flask

Flask provides a simple way to create web servers. It allows you to create a server and define routes, which map URLs to specific Python functions. Let's walk through setting up a basic Flask server.

1. **Install Flask**: You can install Flask using Python's package manager `pip`. Run the following command:

```bash
pip install flask
```

2. **Creating a Simple Flask App**: Here's an example of a very basic Flask app:

```python
from flask import Flask

app = Flask(__name__)

@app.route('/')
def home():
    return 'Hello, World!'

if __name__ == '__main__':
    app.run(debug=True)
```

   o   The `Flask` class is instantiated with the name of the current module (`__name__`), and a Flask app object is created.

   o   The `@app.route('/')` decorator maps the root URL (/) to the `home()` function, which returns a simple string message.

- o The `app.run(debug=True)` line starts the web server in debug mode, which automatically reloads the server when code changes.

3. **Running the Flask App**: Save this code in a file called `app.py`, then run it using the following command:

```bash
```

```bash
python app.py
```

- o The server will start at `http://127.0.0.1:5000/`, and you can visit this URL in your browser to see the "Hello, World!" message.

Building a Simple Web Application with Django

Django provides a more structured approach to web development. Let's walk through creating a simple Django project and application.

1. **Install Django**: To install Django, use the following command:

```bash
```

```bash
pip install django
```

2. **Create a Django Project**: To start a new Django project, run the following command:

```bash
bash
```

```bash
django-admin startproject myproject
```

This will create a directory named `myproject` with the necessary files and folder structure for a Django project.

3. **Create a Django App**: In Django, an app is a modular component of the project that handles a specific piece of functionality. To create a new app, navigate into the project directory and run:

```bash
bash
```

```bash
python manage.py startapp blog
```

This will create a `blog` directory inside the `myproject` directory.

4. **Define a Simple View**: Inside the `blog/views.py` file, define a simple view that will return a message when accessed via the web browser:

```python
python
```

```python
from django.http import HttpResponse

def home(request):
    return HttpResponse("Welcome to the Blog Home Page!")
```

5. **Map the View to a URL**: In Django, URL patterns are defined in the `urls.py` file. Open the `myproject/urls.py` file and add the route for the `home` view:

python

```python
from django.contrib import admin
from django.urls import path
from blog import views

urlpatterns = [
    path('admin/', admin.site.urls),
    path('', views.home, name='home'),
]
```

6. **Run the Django Server**: To start the Django development server, run the following command:

bash

```bash
python manage.py runserver
```

The server will start at `http://127.0.0.1:8000/`, and visiting this URL in the browser will display the "Welcome to the Blog Home Page!" message.

Real-World Example: A Blog Application Using Django and Python

Now that we've learned the basics of both Flask and Django, let's build a simple blog application using Django. The blog will allow users to view and create posts.

1. **Defining the Model**: In Django, models define the structure of the database. Let's create a simple model for blog posts. In `blog/models.py`:

python

```python
from django.db import models

class Post(models.Model):
    title = models.CharField(max_length=100)
    content = models.TextField()
    created_at                      =
models.DateTimeField(auto_now_add=True)

    def __str__(self):
        return self.title
```

2. **Create the Database Table**: Django uses migrations to manage database changes. After defining the model, run the following commands to create the database table:

bash

```bash
python manage.py makemigrations
python manage.py migrate
```

3. **Admin Interface**: Django comes with a built-in admin interface to manage your data. To enable the `Post` model in the admin interface, register it in `blog/admin.py`:

python

```python
from django.contrib import admin
from .models import Post

admin.site.register(Post)
```

4. **Creating Views**: In `blog/views.py`, create views to display and add blog posts. For the blog home page, use a function to display all posts:

python

```python
from django.shortcuts import render
from .models import Post

def home(request):
    posts = Post.objects.all()
    return      render(request,      'home.html',
{'posts': posts})

def add_post(request):
    if request.method == "POST":
        title = request.POST['title']
        content = request.POST['content']
```

```
        Post.objects.create(title=title,
content=content)
        return render(request, 'add_post.html')
```

5. **Creating Templates**: Create templates to render the content. In the `blog/templates` folder, create `home.html` and `add_post.html`:

   o **home.html**:

   ```html
   html

   <h1>Blog Posts</h1>
   <ul>
       {% for post in posts %}
           <li>{{    post.title    }}:    {{
   post.content }}</li>
       {% endfor %}
   </ul>
   <a href="/add_post/">Add a New Post</a>
   ```

   o **add_post.html**:

   ```html
   html

   <h1>Add a New Post</h1>
   <form method="post">
       {% csrf_token %}
       <input    type="text"    name="title"
   placeholder="Title" required><br>
   ```

```
        <textarea              name="content"
    placeholder="Content"
    required></textarea><br>
        <button type="submit">Submit</button>
    </form>
```

6. **Mapping Views to URLs**: In `blog/urls.py`, map the views to URLs:

`python`

```
from django.urls import path
from . import views

urlpatterns = [
    path('', views.home, name='home'),
    path('add_post/',              views.add_post,
name='add_post'),
]
```

7. **Running the Blog Application**: Run the Django server again, and visit `http://127.0.0.1:8000/` to view the blog home page. You can add new posts through the `/add_post/` page, and the posts will be displayed on the home page.

Summary

In this chapter, we introduced two major Python web frameworks: Flask and Django. We covered setting up a simple web server with Flask and building a simple web application with Django. We also implemented a real-world blog application using Django, learning how to work with models, views, templates, and the Django admin interface. Understanding these frameworks is essential for modern web development with Python, and both Flask and Django are powerful tools for building scalable and maintainable web applications.

Chapter 14: JavaScript for Frontend Development: DOM Manipulation and Events

Introduction to the Document Object Model (DOM) in JavaScript

The **Document Object Model (DOM)** is an essential concept in frontend web development. It represents the structure of an HTML document as an object-oriented tree structure, where each element, attribute, and piece of text is a node that can be accessed and manipulated using JavaScript. Through the DOM, JavaScript can dynamically alter the content, structure, and style of a web page without requiring a page reload.

The DOM can be thought of as a live, programmable interface to the HTML document. It allows developers to interact with the page by selecting elements, modifying their properties, adding new elements, and deleting existing ones.

1. **DOM Structure**:
   - The DOM represents the entire structure of an HTML document as a hierarchical tree. Each element in the HTML is a node in this tree.
   - For example, consider the following HTML:

```
html
```

```html
<html>
    <body>
        <div id="container">
            <h1>My Webpage</h1>
            <p>Welcome to my website!</p>
        </div>
    </body>
</html>
```

The DOM representation of this HTML document would look like this:

```less
less
```

```
- html
  - body
    - div (id="container")
      - h1
      - p
```

2. **Interacting with the DOM**:

   o JavaScript provides methods to interact with the DOM, such as `getElementById()`, `querySelector()`, and `getElementsByClassName()`.

   o Using these methods, developers can retrieve HTML elements and modify their content, style, or structure dynamically.

Example:

```
javascript
```

```
const title = document.getElementById("title");
title.textContent = "Updated Title";  // Updates
the text content of the element with id "title"
```

In this example, `getElementById("title")` fetches the HTML element with the id `title`, and the `textContent` property is used to change the text of that element.

Handling Events and User Interactions on a Webpage

Events are a crucial part of web development because they allow the web page to respond to user actions such as clicks, keypresses, or mouse movements. JavaScript can be used to listen for these events and execute specific functions when they occur.

1. **Event Listeners**:
   - Event listeners are functions that are executed in response to specific events.
   - The `addEventListener()` method is used to attach an event listener to an element. The syntax is as follows:

```
javascript
```

```
element.addEventListener('event', function);
```

o For example, listening for a button click:

javascript

```
const              button              =
document.getElementById("myButton");
button.addEventListener('click', function() {
    alert("Button was clicked!");
});
```

2. **Common Event Types**:
   o **click**: Fired when the user clicks on an element.
   o **mouseover**: Fired when the mouse pointer enters an element.
   o **keydown**: Fired when a key is pressed down.
   o **submit**: Fired when a form is submitted.
   o **change**: Fired when the value of an input field changes.

3. **Event Object**:
   o The event object provides additional information about the event that occurred. For example, it can give details about the element that triggered the event or the mouse position when the event was triggered.

   Example:

javascript

```
button.addEventListener('click', function(event)
{
    console.log(event.target);    // Logs the
element that was clicked
});
```

4. **Event Delegation**:

   o Event delegation is a technique where events are handled by a parent element rather than individual child elements. This is useful for handling events dynamically for elements that may not yet exist when the page loads.

   o This is typically used with event types like `click`, `submit`, and `change`.

Example:

javascript

```
const            list            =
document.getElementById("todoList");
list.addEventListener('click', function(event) {
    if (event.target.tagName === "LI") {
        alert("Item    clicked:    "    +
event.target.textContent);
    }
});
```

In this example, the event listener is attached to the parent `<ul>` element, and it listens for clicks on any `<li>` elements that exist inside the list.

Real-World Example: Building a To-Do List with JavaScript
Now, let's apply our knowledge of DOM manipulation and events by building a simple to-do list web application. This to-do list will allow users to add items, mark them as complete, and delete items.

1. **HTML Structure**:

    ```html
    html

    <html>
        <body>
            <h1>My To-Do List</h1>
            <input    type="text"    id="todoInput"
    placeholder="Enter a new task">
            <button id="addButton">Add Task</button>
            <ul id="todoList"></ul>
        </body>
    </html>
    ```

2. **JavaScript to Handle DOM Manipulation and Events**:

    ```javascript
    javascript

    // Select  the  input,  button,  and  todo  list
    elements
    ```

```
const              todoInput              =
document.getElementById("todoInput");
const              addButton              =
document.getElementById("addButton");
const              todoList               =
document.getElementById("todoList");


// Event listener to add a new task when the
button is clicked
addButton.addEventListener("click", function() {
    const taskText = todoInput.value;  // Get the
value from the input field
    if (taskText !== "") {   // Ensure that the
input is not empty
        const              newItem              =
document.createElement("li");   // Create a new
<li> element
        newItem.textContent = taskText;   // Set
the text content of the new item


        // Add an event listener to mark the task
as complete when clicked
        newItem.addEventListener("click",
function() {
            newItem.style.textDecoration       =
"line-through";   // Mark as complete
        });


        // Add an event listener to delete the
task when double-clicked
```

CODE CRAFTING: THE COMPLETE GUIDE TO MODERN PROGRAMMING LANGUAGES

```
        newItem.addEventListener("dblclick",
function() {
            todoList.removeChild(newItem);    //
Remove the item from the list
        });


        todoList.appendChild(newItem);    // Add
the new item to the list
        todoInput.value = "";  // Clear the input
field
    }
});
```

Explanation:

- o The addButton is wired up to add new tasks to the to-do list when clicked.
- o When the button is clicked, a new <li> element is created, containing the text from the input field.
- o Event listeners are added to the new list item: one for marking the task as complete when clicked (using textDecoration: line-through) and another for deleting the task when double-clicked (dblclick event).
- o The new item is appended to the <ul> list, and the input field is cleared.

3. **Final Application Behavior**:

- o The user can add tasks to the to-do list by typing in the input field and clicking the "Add Task" button.
- o Tasks can be marked as complete by clicking on them, which will strike through the task text.
- o Tasks can be deleted by double-clicking on them.

4. **Resulting Output**:

- o The page will display a list of tasks. As tasks are added, the list dynamically updates. Clicking a task strikes it out, and double-clicking removes the task from the list.

Best Practices for Writing Interactive, Responsive Web Pages

1. **Keep the User Interface Responsive**:

- o Ensure your web page responds to user interactions without unnecessary delays. Use event listeners to handle user inputs such as clicks, form submissions, and keystrokes.
- o Consider using **debouncing** and **throttling** techniques for performance-heavy events like scrolling or typing.

2. **Use CSS for Visual Feedback**:

- o Use CSS classes to provide visual feedback when an element is clicked or hovered over. This enhances the user experience and gives instant feedback.
- o For example, when a task is marked as completed in the to-do list, you could change its background color or apply a strike-through effect using CSS.

3. **Separate JavaScript from HTML**:

- o While inline event handlers (like `onclick="someFunction()"`) are convenient, it's a best practice to separate your JavaScript logic from your HTML code by using `addEventListener()` and placing JavaScript in a separate file.

4. **Validate User Input**:

- o Always validate user input before using it in your application. For example, in the to-do list, we check whether the input field is empty before adding a new task.

5. **Ensure Accessibility**:

- o Make sure your web applications are accessible to users with disabilities. Use semantic HTML elements, such as buttons and form elements, and provide keyboard accessibility for all interactive elements.

6. **Optimize Performance**:

   o When working with dynamic content, minimize the number of DOM manipulations. Group multiple changes together using `documentFragment` or `innerHTML` for batch updates to improve performance.

Summary

In this chapter, we explored the **Document Object Model (DOM)** and its critical role in frontend web development. We learned how JavaScript allows us to manipulate HTML elements, handle events, and create interactive web applications. By building a simple to-do list, we demonstrated how to use DOM manipulation and event handling to create a responsive user interface. We also covered best practices for writing efficient, accessible, and maintainable web pages. Mastering these techniques will enable you to create rich, interactive web applications that respond to user input in real time.

Chapter 15: Backend Development with JavaScript: Node.js

Introduction to Node.js for Server-Side JavaScript

Node.js is an open-source, cross-platform runtime environment that allows developers to run JavaScript on the server side. It's built on the V8 JavaScript engine (the same engine used by Google Chrome) and is designed to be lightweight, efficient, and capable of handling asynchronous I/O operations, which makes it perfect for scalable, high-performance applications like web servers, APIs, and real-time services.

Before Node.js, JavaScript was primarily used in the browser for client-side scripting. With Node.js, JavaScript can be used to build server-side applications, providing a unified language for both frontend and backend development. This ability to write full-stack JavaScript applications offers many advantages, including shared code, faster development cycles, and the ability to leverage the vast number of libraries in the npm (Node Package Manager) ecosystem.

1. **Asynchronous Nature**:
    - Node.js uses non-blocking, event-driven architecture, meaning it handles I/O operations like reading from disk or querying a database asynchronously. This allows Node.js to handle

many simultaneous connections efficiently without being slowed down by slow I/O operations.

2. **Single-Threaded Model**:

   o While Node.js operates on a single thread, its non-blocking nature enables it to manage many connections concurrently, making it ideal for I/O-heavy tasks. For CPU-intensive tasks, Node.js can utilize multiple threads using worker threads or by delegating the work to other systems.

3. **npm (Node Package Manager)**:

   o npm is the largest ecosystem of open-source libraries and modules, which makes it easy to extend the functionality of your application with reusable code. Whether you need authentication, web frameworks, or data validation, npm provides a rich repository of packages to enhance your development workflow.

Setting Up a Basic Server Using Node.js

To start working with Node.js, the first step is to install Node.js on your machine. Node.js comes with npm pre-installed, so you will be able to access thousands of libraries right out of the box.

1. **Install Node.js**:
    - You can download Node.js from the <u>official Node.js website</u>. Choose the version that matches your operating system, and follow the installation instructions.

2. **Creating a Basic Server**:
    - Once Node.js is installed, you can start writing server-side code in JavaScript. Here's how to set up a basic web server using the built-in `http` module in Node.js.

Example:

```javascript
const http = require('http');  // Import the http module

const server = http.createServer((req, res) => {
    res.statusCode = 200;  // Set the status code to 200 (OK)
    res.setHeader('Content-Type', 'text/plain');  // Set the response header
    res.end('Hello, World!\n');  // Send the response message
});

const port = 3000;  // Set the port number
```

```
server.listen(port, () => {
    console.log(`Server          running          at
http://localhost:${port}/`);
});
```

- o This code creates a simple HTTP server that listens on port 3000. When you visit `http://localhost:3000/` in your browser, you'll see "Hello, World!" displayed.

3. **Running the Server**:
   - o Save the code in a file called `server.js` and run the following command in the terminal:

```bash
```

```
node server.js
```

   - o You should see the message `Server running at` `http://localhost:3000/` in the terminal. Visiting this URL in your browser will show the "Hello, World!" message.

4. **Handling Different Routes**:
   - o You can enhance this server by handling different routes using basic JavaScript conditions. For example:

```javascript
```

```
const http = require('http');

const server = http.createServer((req, res) => {
    if (req.url === '/') {
        res.statusCode = 200;
        res.setHeader('Content-Type',
'text/plain');
        res.end('Welcome to the Homepage!');
    } else if (req.url === '/about') {
        res.statusCode = 200;
        res.setHeader('Content-Type',
'text/plain');
        res.end('This is the About page');
    } else {
        res.statusCode = 404;
        res.setHeader('Content-Type',
'text/plain');
        res.end('Page Not Found');
    }
});

const port = 3000;
server.listen(port, () => {
    console.log(`Server          running          at
http://localhost:${port}/`);
});
```

o This server now handles different routes like
`/about` and returns different content for each
URL path.

Working with Databases Using JavaScript (MongoDB, SQL)

Node.js is versatile and can be integrated with both **NoSQL**
databases like MongoDB and **SQL** databases like MySQL or
PostgreSQL. The choice of database depends on your application's
requirements.

1. **MongoDB with Node.js**:
   o **MongoDB** is a popular NoSQL database that
   stores data in a flexible, JSON-like format called
   BSON. MongoDB is commonly used with
   Node.js for web applications that need scalable
   and schema-less storage.

Setting up MongoDB:

   o Install MongoDB and the `mongodb` Node.js driver:

   ```bash
   bash
   ```

   ```bash
   npm install mongodb
   ```
Example of Connecting to MongoDB:

```javascript
javascript
```

```javascript
const { MongoClient } = require('mongodb');

const url = 'mongodb://localhost:27017';
const dbName = 'mydatabase';

async function main() {
    const client = new MongoClient(url);
    await client.connect();
    console.log('Connected to MongoDB');

    const db = client.db(dbName);
    const collection = db.collection('users');

    // Insert a document
    await collection.insertOne({ name: 'John
Doe', age: 30 });

    // Find the inserted document
    const user = await collection.findOne({ name:
'John Doe' });
    console.log(user);

    await client.close();
}

main().catch(console.error);
```

- o **This example connects to a local MongoDB server, inserts a document into the** users collection, retrieves it, and logs the result to the console.

2. **SQL Database (MySQL) with Node.js**:
   - For relational data, **MySQL** is a widely used SQL database. You can interact with MySQL from Node.js using the `mysql2` package.

Setting up MySQL:

   - Install the MySQL driver:

   ```bash
   bash
   ```

   ```bash
   npm install mysql2
   ```

Example of Connecting to MySQL:

```javascript
javascript

const mysql = require('mysql2');

// Create a connection to the database
const connection = mysql.createConnection({
    host: 'localhost',
    user: 'root',
    password: 'yourpassword',
    database: 'mydatabase'
});

connection.connect((err) => {
```

```
    if (err) {
        console.error('Error connecting to the
database:', err.stack);
        return;
    }
    console.log('Connected to MySQL database');
});

// Run a query
connection.query('SELECT * FROM users', (err,
results) => {
    if (err) throw err;
    console.log(results);
});

// Close the connection
connection.end();
```

> o   This example connects to a MySQL database,
> runs a query to fetch all records from the `users`
> table, and logs the results to the console.

Real-World Example: Building a Simple API with Node.js

In this section, we'll build a simple API using **Express**, a web application framework for Node.js. The API will provide endpoints to handle basic CRUD operations for a list of users.

1. **Install Express**:
   o   Install the Express package:

```bash
bash

npm install express
```

2. **Building the API**:

```javascript
javascript

const express = require('express');
const app = express();
const port = 3000;

// Middleware to parse JSON requests
app.use(express.json());

// In-memory users database (can be replaced by
MongoDB or MySQL)
let users = [
    { id: 1, name: 'Alice', age: 25 },
    { id: 2, name: 'Bob', age: 30 },
];

// Get all users
app.get('/users', (req, res) => {
    res.json(users);
});

// Get a user by ID
app.get('/users/:id', (req, res) => {
    const user = users.find(u => u.id ===
parseInt(req.params.id));
```

```
    if (!user) return res.status(404).send('User
not found');
    res.json(user);
});

// Create a new user
app.post('/users', (req, res) => {
    const { name, age } = req.body;
    const newUser = {
        id: users.length + 1,
        name,
        age,
    };
    users.push(newUser);
    res.status(201).json(newUser);
});

// Update an existing user
app.put('/users/:id', (req, res) => {
    const user = users.find(u => u.id ===
parseInt(req.params.id));
    if (!user) return res.status(404).send('User
not found');

    user.name = req.body.name;
    user.age = req.body.age;
    res.json(user);
});

// Delete a user
app.delete('/users/:id', (req, res) => {
```

```
    const userIndex = users.findIndex(u => u.id
=== parseInt(req.params.id));
    if    (userIndex    ===    -1)    return
res.status(404).send('User not found');

    users.splice(userIndex, 1);
    res.status(204).send();
});


// Start the server
app.listen(port, () => {
    console.log(`API    is    running    at
http://localhost:${port}/`);
});
```

3. **Running the API**:

   o To run the server, save the code in a file named `app.js` and run the following command:

   ```bash
   node app.js
   ```

   o This will start an API server that listens on `http://localhost:3000`. You can test the various routes using Postman or any API client.

Summary

In this chapter, we learned about **Node.js**, a powerful runtime environment that allows us to use JavaScript for backend development. We explored setting up a basic server using Node.js, handling requests with Express, and working with databases like MongoDB and MySQL. We then built a simple REST API that performs CRUD operations. Node.js and its ecosystem of packages make it easy to build scalable and efficient web applications with JavaScript on both the frontend and backend.

Chapter 16: Working with Databases in Python, JavaScript, and C++

Introduction to Relational and NoSQL Databases

Databases are critical for storing and managing data in modern applications. There are two primary types of databases: **Relational databases (SQL)** and **NoSQL databases**. Understanding when to use each type can greatly impact the performance, scalability, and flexibility of your application.

1. **Relational Databases (SQL)**:

    o **SQL (Structured Query Language)** databases are based on a structured schema that organizes data into tables with rows and columns. These databases are ideal for applications that require a fixed schema, transactions, and complex queries involving joins, constraints, and aggregations.

    o **Examples**: MySQL, PostgreSQL, SQLite, SQL Server, Oracle.

    Key Features:

- o **ACID Properties**: Atomicity, Consistency, Isolation, Durability, which ensure data integrity during transactions.
- o **Schema**: A predefined structure where tables and relationships between data are defined.

2. **NoSQL Databases**:

- o **NoSQL** databases are designed for flexible, scalable storage. They do not require a predefined schema and are often used for large-scale applications where data is less structured or changes frequently. These databases can handle a wide variety of data models, such as key-value pairs, document-based, column-family, or graph-based data.
- o **Examples**: MongoDB, Cassandra, Redis, Couchbase, DynamoDB.

Key Features:

- o **Schema-less**: Data is not confined to a rigid structure.
- o **Scalability**: NoSQL databases are designed to scale out by distributing data across multiple machines.

- o **High Availability**: Many NoSQL databases are designed to offer better availability and partition tolerance (CAP theorem).

Using SQLite with Python for Small Projects

SQLite is a lightweight, self-contained relational database engine that is ideal for small projects and applications where simplicity, minimal configuration, and embedded database solutions are needed. It is a file-based database that doesn't require a separate server process, making it easy to set up and use in small applications.

1. **Installing SQLite in Python**:
   - o Python's `sqlite3` module provides a straightforward interface to SQLite databases, and it is included in the standard Python library, so no additional installation is required.
2. **Creating a Database and Connecting**:
   - o Let's create a simple SQLite database for a product inventory system and perform some basic operations, like creating tables and inserting data.

Example:

```python

import sqlite3
```

```python
# Create or connect to a database
connection = sqlite3.connect('inventory.db')

# Create a cursor object to interact with the
database
cursor = connection.cursor()

# Create a table for storing products
cursor.execute('''
    CREATE TABLE IF NOT EXISTS products (
        id INTEGER PRIMARY KEY AUTOINCREMENT,
        name TEXT NOT NULL,
        quantity INTEGER,
        price REAL
    )
''')

# Insert a new product
cursor.execute('''
    INSERT INTO products (name, quantity, price)
    VALUES ('Laptop', 50, 799.99)
''')

# Commit the changes and close the connection
connection.commit()

# Query the database
cursor.execute('SELECT * FROM products')
rows = cursor.fetchall()
```

```
for row in rows:
    print(row)


connection.close()
```

Explanation:

o The `sqlite3.connect('inventory.db')` function creates a new SQLite database file named `inventory.db`.

o The `CREATE TABLE` statement defines a table to store products with columns for the product's name, quantity, and price.

o The `INSERT INTO` statement adds a new product to the table.

o The `SELECT * FROM products` query retrieves all records from the `products` table and prints them.

o The database is saved in a file, and the connection is closed with `connection.close()`.

Integrating MongoDB with JavaScript (Node.js)

MongoDB is a popular NoSQL database known for its flexibility, scalability, and performance. In Node.js, the `mongodb` package can be used to interact with MongoDB. This section will show you how to set up MongoDB in a Node.js application and perform basic database operations.

1. **Setting Up MongoDB**:
   - You will need to install MongoDB on your machine, or you can use a cloud service like **MongoDB Atlas**.
   - To use MongoDB with Node.js, you need to install the `mongodb` package. Run the following command:

   ```bash
   npm install mongodb
   ```

2. **Connecting to MongoDB**:
   - You can connect to a local MongoDB instance or a cloud-based instance with MongoDB Atlas. Let's connect to a MongoDB database and perform CRUD operations.

   Example:

   ```javascript
   const { MongoClient } = require('mongodb');

   const url = 'mongodb://localhost:27017';   // MongoDB connection URL
   const dbName = 'inventory';
   ```

```javascript
async function main() {
    const client = new MongoClient(url);

    try {
        // Connect to the MongoDB server
        await client.connect();
        console.log('Connected to MongoDB');

        // Get the database and collection
        const db = client.db(dbName);
        const collection =
db.collection('products');

        // Insert a new product
        const product = {
            name: 'Smartphone',
            quantity: 100,
            price: 499.99,
        };
        await collection.insertOne(product);
        console.log('Product inserted');

        // Find all products
        const products = await
collection.find().toArray();
        console.log('Products:', products);
    } finally {
        await client.close();
    }
}
```

```
main().catch(console.error);
```

Explanation:

- `MongoClient.connect()` establishes a connection to MongoDB.
- The `insertOne()` method inserts a new product into the `products` collection.
- `find().toArray()` retrieves all products from the collection and logs them to the console.
- The `await` keyword ensures that asynchronous operations like database connections and queries are completed before proceeding.

Real-World Example: Building a Product Inventory System with Database Integration

Now, let's combine the concepts from Python and JavaScript to build a simple product inventory system that can store, update, and retrieve product data using a database.

1. **Python Example (SQLite)**: Here, we will expand the inventory system built with SQLite by adding functionality to update and delete products, as well as to handle multiple products efficiently.

Example:

```python
python
```

```python
import sqlite3

def create_table():
    connection = sqlite3.connect('inventory.db')
    cursor = connection.cursor()
    cursor.execute('''
        CREATE TABLE IF NOT EXISTS products (
            id INTEGER PRIMARY KEY AUTOINCREMENT,
            name TEXT NOT NULL,
            quantity INTEGER,
            price REAL
        )
    ''')
    connection.commit()
    connection.close()

def insert_product(name, quantity, price):
    connection = sqlite3.connect('inventory.db')
    cursor = connection.cursor()
    cursor.execute('''
        INSERT INTO products (name, quantity, price)
        VALUES (?, ?, ?)
    ''', (name, quantity, price))
    connection.commit()
    connection.close()

def update_product(id, name, quantity, price):
    connection = sqlite3.connect('inventory.db')
```

```python
    cursor = connection.cursor()
    cursor.execute('''
        UPDATE products
        SET name = ?, quantity = ?, price = ?
        WHERE id = ?
    ''', (name, quantity, price, id))
    connection.commit()
    connection.close()

def delete_product(id):
    connection = sqlite3.connect('inventory.db')
    cursor = connection.cursor()
    cursor.execute('''
        DELETE FROM products WHERE id = ?
    ''', (id,))
    connection.commit()
    connection.close()

def list_products():
    connection = sqlite3.connect('inventory.db')
    cursor = connection.cursor()
    cursor.execute('SELECT * FROM products')
    rows = cursor.fetchall()
    for row in rows:
        print(row)
    connection.close()

# Example Usage
create_table()
insert_product('Laptop', 50, 799.99)
insert_product('Smartphone', 100, 499.99)
```

```
list_products()
update_product(1, 'Laptop', 40, 749.99)
delete_product(2)
list_products()
```

Explanation:

- o This code demonstrates how to add, update, and delete products from the SQLite database.
- o The `insert_product`, `update_product`, and `delete_product` functions allow us to perform CRUD operations on the `products` table.

2. **JavaScript Example (MongoDB)**: Similarly, we can implement a product inventory system in Node.js using MongoDB. This system will allow us to store products, update their details, and delete them from the MongoDB collection.

Example:

```javascript
const { MongoClient } = require('mongodb');

const url = 'mongodb://localhost:27017';
const dbName = 'inventory';
const client = new MongoClient(url);

async function main() {
    try {
```

```
        await client.connect();
        console.log('Connected to MongoDB');
        const db = client.db(dbName);
        const            collection            =
db.collection('products');

        // Insert a new product
        await    collection.insertOne({    name:
'Tablet', quantity: 80, price: 299.99 });

        // Update an existing product
        await    collection.updateOne({    name:
'Tablet' }, { $set: { price: 279.99 } });

        // Delete a product
        await    collection.deleteOne({    name:
'Tablet' });

        // List all products
        const        products        =        await
collection.find().toArray();
        console.log(products);
    } finally {
        await client.close();
    }
}

main().catch(console.error);
```

Explanation:

- o This code connects to MongoDB and allows you to insert, update, and delete products in the `products` **collection.**

- o **The** `insertOne`, `updateOne`, **and** `deleteOne` methods perform the CRUD operations, and the `find().toArray()` method retrieves all products from the collection.

Summary

In this chapter, we learned how to work with both **relational (SQLite)** and **NoSQL (MongoDB)** databases in Python and JavaScript (Node.js). We explored how to set up databases, perform CRUD operations, and integrate databases into applications. We also demonstrated a real-world example by building a product inventory system in both Python and JavaScript, which highlights the key concepts of working with databases in these languages. Understanding how to integrate databases with your applications is crucial for developing dynamic and data-driven systems.

Chapter 17: Advanced Topics in Python: Decorators, Generators, and Context Managers

Introduction to Advanced Python Features: Decorators, Generators, and Context Managers

Python is a versatile and expressive programming language that supports a wide array of advanced programming concepts and features. These features, such as **decorators**, **generators**, and **context managers**, enable developers to write more efficient, readable, and maintainable code. In this chapter, we'll explore these three advanced features, demonstrate their uses with real-world examples, and show how Python's built-in libraries can enhance functionality.

1. **Decorators**:
    - A **decorator** is a design pattern in Python that allows you to modify or extend the behavior of a function or method without changing its source code. Decorators are often used to add functionality such as logging, access control, or performance monitoring, among other things.
    - A decorator is typically a function that takes another function as an argument and returns a

new function that adds some additional behavior.

2. **Generators**:

    o **Generators** are a special kind of iterator in Python. Instead of returning a single value, they use the `yield` keyword to return multiple values one at a time, allowing for lazy evaluation. Generators are particularly useful for handling large datasets or streams of data where you don't want to load everything into memory at once.

3. **Context Managers**:

    o A **context manager** in Python is used to manage resources (like file handles, network connections, or locks) within a specific context. The most common use case is with the `with` statement, which ensures that resources are properly acquired and released. This is particularly useful when working with external resources that need to be cleaned up after use (e.g., closing files, releasing database connections).

1. Decorators: Adding Functionality to Functions

A **decorator** is a function that modifies the behavior of another function. This is often used for cross-cutting concerns such as logging, authentication, and caching, without modifying the function itself.

1. **Basic Decorator Syntax**: Decorators are usually defined using the @decorator_name syntax and are applied to functions or methods.

   Example:

   python

   ```python
   def simple_decorator(func):
       def wrapper():
           print("Before the function is called.")
           func()
           print("After the function is called.")
       return wrapper

   @simple_decorator
   def say_hello():
       print("Hello!")

   say_hello()
   ```

   Explanation:

   o simple_decorator is a decorator that takes a function (func) as an argument.

- o The `wrapper` function adds functionality before and after calling the original function (`func()`).
- o When you call `say_hello()`, the output is:

```vbnet
Before the function is called.
Hello!
After the function is called.
```

2. **Using Decorators with Arguments**: Decorators can also accept arguments by creating a decorator that returns another function.

Example:

```python
def repeat(n):
    def decorator(func):
        def wrapper(*args, **kwargs):
            for _ in range(n):
                result = func(*args, **kwargs)
            return result
        return wrapper
    return decorator

@repeat(3)
def greet(name):
    print(f"Hello, {name}!")
```

```
greet("Alice")
```

Explanation:

- o The `repeat` decorator takes an argument `n`, which determines how many times to call the decorated function.
- o In this example, `greet` is called three times with the name "Alice", so the output is:

```
Hello, Alice!
Hello, Alice!
Hello, Alice!
```

2. Generators: Efficient Iteration with Yield

A **generator** is a function that produces a sequence of values over time, using the `yield` keyword. Instead of returning a complete list or other data structure, a generator produces values one at a time, which is more memory-efficient for large datasets.

1. **Basic Generator Example**: Here's how to define a simple generator function using `yield`:

```python
def count_up_to(max):
    count = 1
    while count <= max:
```

```
        yield count
        count += 1

counter = count_up_to(5)
for number in counter:
    print(number)
```

Explanation:

- The count_up_to function is a generator that yields numbers from 1 to the specified max.
- When the for loop is executed, it iterates over the generator, calling yield each time to return a new value.

2. **Using Generators for Large Datasets**: Generators are ideal for iterating over large datasets without loading everything into memory. For example, when processing large files, a generator can read one line at a time.

Example: Reading a file line-by-line using a generator:

python

```
def read_file(file_name):
    with open(file_name, 'r') as file:
        for line in file:
            yield line.strip()

for line in read_file("large_file.txt"):
    print(line)
```

Explanation:

- The `read_file` generator yields each line of the file, one by one, rather than reading the entire file into memory at once.
- This is particularly useful for reading very large files.

3. Context Managers: Managing Resources

A **context manager** is used to manage the setup and cleanup of resources, typically when working with external resources like files, network connections, or database connections. The `with` statement is used to wrap the code that acquires and releases the resource.

1. **Using the `with` Statement**: A typical use case for context managers is working with files. The `with` statement ensures that the file is properly opened and closed after use.

   Example:

   python

   ```python
   with open('file.txt', 'r') as file:
       content = file.read()
       print(content)
   ```
   Explanation:

- o The `with` statement automatically handles the opening and closing of the file, ensuring that resources are properly cleaned up (e.g., the file is closed even if an exception occurs).
- o This reduces the chances of errors such as file handles being left open.

2. **Creating a Custom Context Manager**: You can create your own context manager by implementing the `__enter__()` and `__exit__()` methods in a class.

Example:

python

```python
class Timer:
    def __enter__(self):
        import time
        self.start_time = time.time()
        return self

    def __exit__(self, exc_type, exc_value, traceback):
        import time
        self.end_time = time.time()
        self.duration = self.end_time - self.start_time
        print(f"Execution time: {self.duration:.4f} seconds")
```

```python
with Timer() as timer:
    # Simulate a task
    sum(range(1, 1000000))

# Output: Execution time: 0.0734 seconds
```

Explanation:

- The `Timer` class measures the time it takes to execute the code inside the `with` block.
- The `__enter__()` method starts the timer, and the `__exit__()` method stops the timer and prints the duration.

Real-World Example: Optimizing Code with Decorators and Generators

Let's say we want to build a data processing pipeline that involves performing multiple transformations on a dataset. We can use **decorators** for logging and **generators** for efficient data processing.

1. **Using a Decorator for Logging**: We'll define a decorator to log function execution time and other relevant information.

   Example:

   ```python
   python

   import time
   ```

```
def log_function_call(func):
    def wrapper(*args, **kwargs):
        start_time = time.time()
        result = func(*args, **kwargs)
        end_time = time.time()
        print(f"Function          {func.__name__}
executed in {end_time - start_time:.4f} seconds")
        return result
    return wrapper


@log_function_call
def process_data(data):
    total = 0
    for item in data:
        total += item
    return total


data = range(1, 100000)
result = process_data(data)
```

Explanation:

- o The `log_function_call` decorator logs the execution time of the `process_data` function.
- o The decorator is applied to `process_data` with the `@log_function_call` syntax.

2. **Using a Generator for Efficient Data Processing**: We can use a generator to process large datasets without loading everything into memory at once.

Example:

```python
python

def generate_data():
    for i in range(1, 100000):
        yield i

def process_large_data():
    total = 0
    for value in generate_data():
        total += value
    return total

result = process_large_data()
print(result)
```

Explanation:

- ○ `generate_data` is a generator that yields values one by one.

- ○ `process_large_data` processes the values generated by `generate_data`, allowing us to handle large datasets efficiently without loading everything into memory at once.

How to Use Python's Built-in Libraries for Advanced Functionality

Python provides a rich set of built-in libraries for advanced functionality. Here are some key libraries that enhance the capability of decorators, generators, and context managers:

1. `functools`:
   - Contains utilities for functional programming, including `wraps` for preserving the metadata of functions when decorating them.
   - Example: `functools.lru_cache` can be used to memoize function results to optimize performance.

2. `itertools`:
   - Provides a set of fast, memory-efficient tools for working with iterators, including `count`, `cycle`, `chain`, and `combinations`.
   - Example: `itertools.islice` allows you to slice iterators without creating a full list in memory.

3. `contextlib`:
   - Provides utilities for creating context managers. The `contextlib.contextmanager` decorator simplifies writing custom context managers.
   - Example: You can create a custom context manager for managing database connections or locks.

Summary

In this chapter, we explored three advanced Python features: **decorators**, **generators**, and **context managers**. We demonstrated how decorators can be used to add functionality to functions, how generators provide efficient ways to handle large datasets, and how context managers help manage resources like file handles and database connections. Additionally, we saw how Python's built-in libraries such as `functools`, `itertools`, and `contextlib` provide advanced functionality to optimize and extend our code. These features make Python an incredibly powerful and flexible language for both small and large-scale projects.

Chapter 18: Asynchronous Programming in JavaScript

Understanding Synchronous vs. Asynchronous Execution

To understand asynchronous programming, it's crucial to first comprehend the difference between **synchronous** and **asynchronous** execution.

1. **Synchronous Execution**:
   - In synchronous programming, tasks are executed one after the other, in a sequential manner. Each task waits for the previous one to finish before it starts executing.
   - If a task takes a long time (like reading a large file or fetching data from a server), it can block the execution of subsequent tasks, leading to performance issues and delays in user interaction.
   - **Example**:

   ```javascript
   console.log("Task 1");
   console.log("Task 2");  // This will not
   run until Task 1 is finished.
   ```

2. **Asynchronous Execution**:
   - In asynchronous programming, tasks are executed independently of the main program flow. The program doesn't wait for a task to finish; instead, it moves on to other tasks. Once the long-running task finishes, a callback or event handler is used to handle the result.
   - This approach is particularly beneficial for I/O-bound tasks (e.g., API requests, file operations) as it allows other tasks to run concurrently without blocking the main thread.
   - **Example**:

```javascript
console.log("Task 1");
setTimeout(() => {
    console.log("Task 2");  // Task 2 runs
asynchronously after a delay
}, 1000);
console.log("Task  3");  // This  runs
immediately after Task 1, not waiting for
Task 2
```

3. In the example above, "Task 3" prints immediately after "Task 1", even though "Task 2" has been scheduled to run asynchronously after a delay.

Using Callbacks, Promises, and Async/Await in JavaScript
JavaScript provides different ways to handle asynchronous code. Below are the most common techniques: **callbacks**, **promises**, and **async/await**.

1. **Callbacks**:
   - A **callback** is a function passed as an argument to another function, which is invoked once the asynchronous task is complete.
   - **Example**:

   javascript

   ```javascript
   function fetchData(callback) {
       setTimeout(() => {
           callback("Data fetched");
       }, 1000);
   }

   fetchData(function(result) {
       console.log(result);   // Output: Data
   fetched
   });
   ```

2. **Callback Hell**:
   - One of the main issues with callbacks is that they can lead to "callback hell" or "pyramid of doom." This happens when you have multiple

nested callbacks, which makes the code hard to read and maintain.

Example of Callback Hell:

```javascript

asyncFunction(function(result) {
    asyncFunction2(function(result2) {
        asyncFunction3(function(result3) {
            console.log(result3);
        });
    });
});
```

3. **Promises:**

   o A **promise** is a modern alternative to callbacks. It represents a value that may be available now, or in the future, or never. Promises have three states: **pending, fulfilled**, or **rejected**.

   o Promises allow you to chain operations in a more readable way using `.then()` and `.catch()` methods.

   o **Example:**

   ```javascript

   function fetchData() {
   ```

```
        return   new   Promise((resolve,   reject)
=>  {
        setTimeout(()  =>  {
            resolve("Data  fetched");
        },  1000);
    });
}


fetchData()
    .then(result  =>  {
        console.log(result);    //  Output:
Data  fetched
    })
    .catch(error  =>  {
        console.log(error);
    });
```

4. **Async/Await**:

   o **async/await** is syntactic sugar built on top of promises that makes asynchronous code look and behave more like synchronous code. The async keyword is used to define an asynchronous function, and await is used to pause the execution until the promise resolves.

   o This approach significantly improves code readability and reduces the complexity of chaining promises.

   o **Example**:

```javascript
async function fetchData() {
    return new Promise((resolve, reject) => {
        setTimeout(() => {
            resolve("Data fetched");
        }, 1000);
    });
}

async function main() {
    const result = await fetchData();
    console.log(result);   // Output: Data fetched
}

main();
```

o **Explanation**:
- `fetchData()` returns a promise.
- Inside the `main()` function, we use `await` to wait for the `fetchData()` promise to resolve, then print the result.

Real-World Example: Fetching Data from an API Asynchronously with JavaScript

In this section, we will use **fetch()**, a modern JavaScript API, to asynchronously fetch data from an external API and handle the response. We'll demonstrate this using **async/await** for simplicity and better readability.

1. **Fetching Data with `fetch()`**:

    o The `fetch()` function is used to make HTTP requests. It returns a promise that resolves to the response of the request.

    Example: Fetching data from a public API (e.g., JSONPlaceholder API):

    ```javascript
    async function getPosts() {
        try {
            const response = await fetch("https://jsonplaceholder.typicode.com/posts");
            if (!response.ok) {
                throw new Error("Network response was not ok");
            }
            const posts = await response.json();
            console.log(posts); // Logs the fetched posts
        } catch (error) {
            console.error("Error fetching data:", error);
        }
    ```

```
}
```

```
getPosts();
```

Explanation:

- o `fetch()` sends an HTTP request to the URL.
- o `await` pauses the execution until the response is received.
- o We use `response.json()` to parse the JSON data from the response.
- o If an error occurs (like a network issue), it's caught in the `catch` block.

2. **Handling Errors**:

- o In asynchronous code, it's important to handle errors properly to prevent issues from crashing the application. Using `try/catch` with `async/await` makes it easy to catch and manage errors.
- o In the example above, if the network response is not OK (e.g., if the server returns a 404 or 500 status code), an error is thrown and caught in the `catch` block.

Tips for Avoiding Callback Hell and Improving Asynchronous Code Readability

1. **Use Promises or Async/Await Instead of Nested Callbacks**:
   - Using **promises** or **async/await** allows for cleaner, more readable asynchronous code by avoiding deeply nested callbacks (callback hell).
2. **Break Down Complex Logic**:
   - If your asynchronous code involves multiple tasks that depend on each other, break down the logic into smaller functions, each with a single responsibility. This makes it easier to follow and debug.

Example: Instead of nesting multiple callbacks inside each other, you can structure your code into smaller, reusable functions:

```javascript
function fetchData() {
    return
fetch('https://api.example.com/data');
}

function processData(response) {
    return response.json();
}

function displayData(data) {
```

```javascript
        console.log(data);
    }


async function main() {
    try {
        const response = await fetchData();
        const       data      =      await
processData(response);
        displayData(data);
    } catch (error) {
        console.error('Error:', error);
    }
}


main();
```

3. **Use `Promise.all()` for Concurrent Asynchronous Operations**:

   o   If you need to execute multiple asynchronous tasks concurrently and wait for all of them to complete, `Promise.all()` is an efficient way to handle this.

Example:

```
javascript


async function fetchDataFromMultipleSources() {
    const               url1               =
'https://api.example.com/data1';
```

```
const                url2                =
'https://api.example.com/data2';

    try {
        const    [data1,    data2]    =    await
Promise.all([fetch(url1), fetch(url2)]);
        const json1 = await data1.json();
        const json2 = await data2.json();
        console.log(json1, json2);
    } catch (error) {
        console.error('Error    fetching    data:',
error);
    }
}


fetchDataFromMultipleSources();
```

4. **Leverage async Functions for Sequential Asynchronous Operations**:

   o When you need to execute asynchronous operations in sequence, using async/await allows you to avoid callback chains and make the code look synchronous while maintaining the non-blocking nature.

5. **Keep the Code DRY (Don't Repeat Yourself)**:

   o Avoid repeating similar logic. If you have multiple asynchronous tasks that look similar, abstract them into a reusable function. This will make your code cleaner and easier to maintain.

Summary

In this chapter, we explored **asynchronous programming** in JavaScript, covering the differences between synchronous and asynchronous execution. We learned how to handle asynchronous tasks using **callbacks**, **promises**, and **async/await**. We also demonstrated how to fetch data from an API asynchronously and handle errors properly. Lastly, we discussed tips for improving asynchronous code readability, including breaking down complex tasks into smaller functions and using `Promise.all()` for concurrent operations.

Mastering asynchronous programming is essential for building efficient, responsive web applications that can handle I/O-bound tasks like API calls, file reading, and network requests without blocking the main execution thread.

Chapter 19: Multithreading and Concurrency in C++

Introduction to Multithreading and Parallelism in C++

In modern applications, especially those that require high performance and responsiveness, **multithreading** and **parallelism** are essential concepts. Multithreading allows a program to execute multiple threads concurrently, taking advantage of multi-core processors, while parallelism refers to executing tasks simultaneously to achieve better performance.

C++ provides robust support for **multithreading** and **concurrency** through the Standard Library, particularly in C++11 and later versions. The introduction of the `<thread>`, `<mutex>`, and `<condition_variable>` libraries allows developers to build efficient, thread-safe, and concurrent programs.

1. **Multithreading**:
    o   Multithreading allows a program to perform multiple tasks at the same time (or seemingly simultaneously). It works by splitting a program's work into separate threads that can run concurrently on different CPU cores or in time-sliced intervals on a single core.

- ○ Each thread runs in its own execution context, but they can share data, leading to potential issues such as race conditions, deadlocks, and inconsistent state. Proper synchronization is required to avoid these problems.

2. **Parallelism**:
   - ○ Parallelism refers to executing multiple tasks simultaneously, where each task runs on its own CPU core. Parallel computing enables applications to scale better on multi-core processors and significantly boosts performance for computationally expensive tasks.
   - ○ Parallelism can be achieved using multiple threads, but not all multithreading problems are inherently parallel (e.g., when tasks depend on the results of others).

Using Threads, Mutexes, and Condition Variables

1. **Threads in C++**:
   - ○ A **thread** represents an independent path of execution within a program. C++ provides the `std::thread` class to create and manage threads.

Basic Thread Creation:

cpp

```cpp
#include <iostream>
#include <thread>

void print_hello() {
    std::cout << "Hello from thread!" << std::endl;
}

int main() {
    // Create a new thread that runs the print_hello function
    std::thread t(print_hello);

    // Join the thread to the main thread
    t.join();

    std::cout << "Hello from main!" << std::endl;
    return 0;
}
```

o   In this example, the `std::thread` class is used to create a new thread that executes the `print_hello` function.

- o The `join()` function ensures that the main thread waits for the created thread to finish before continuing.

2. **Mutexes (Mutual Exclusion)**:
   - o A **mutex** is used to prevent multiple threads from accessing shared resources concurrently, which can lead to data races and corruption. A mutex ensures that only one thread can access the resource at a time.

Example of Using Mutex:

cpp

```cpp
#include <iostream>
#include <thread>
#include <mutex>

std::mutex mtx;

void print_hello() {
    mtx.lock();   // Lock the mutex
    std::cout << "Hello from thread!" << std::endl;
    mtx.unlock();   // Unlock the mutex
}

int main() {
    std::thread t1(print_hello);
```

```
    std::thread t2(print_hello);

    t1.join();
    t2.join();

    return 0;
}
```

Explanation:

- The `std::mutex` object (`mtx`) is used to synchronize access to the `print_hello` function. When one thread locks the mutex, the other thread must wait for it to be unlocked.

3. **Condition Variables**:

   - **Condition variables** are used to synchronize threads by allowing them to wait for certain conditions to be met. A condition variable allows one thread to signal another thread that it can proceed, helping to coordinate the work between threads.

Example of Condition Variables:

cpp

```
#include <iostream>
#include <thread>
#include <mutex>
```

```cpp
#include <condition_variable>

std::mutex mtx;
std::condition_variable cv;
bool ready = false;

void print_hello() {
    std::unique_lock<std::mutex> lock(mtx);
    while (!ready) {  // Wait until ready becomes true
        cv.wait(lock);
    }
    std::cout << "Hello from thread!" << std::endl;
}

void go() {
    std::unique_lock<std::mutex> lock(mtx);
    ready = true;
    cv.notify_all();   // Notify all threads waiting on the condition variable
}

int main() {
    std::thread t1(print_hello);
    std::thread t2(print_hello);

    std::cout << "Preparing..." << std::endl;

    std::this_thread::sleep_for(std::chrono::seconds(1));
```

```
go();   // Signal the threads to proceed

t1.join();
t2.join();

return 0;
}
```

Explanation:

- o The print_hello function waits until the ready variable is true before it proceeds.
- o The go() function sets ready to true and notifies all threads waiting on the condition variable cv to continue.

Real-World Example: Implementing a Multi-Threaded Server in C++

Let's implement a basic multi-threaded server that can handle multiple client connections concurrently. This example demonstrates how to use std::thread, std::mutex, and std::condition_variable to build a simple server that processes multiple client requests in parallel.

Example: Multi-threaded Server:

cpp

```
#include <iostream>
```

```cpp
#include <thread>
#include <vector>
#include <mutex>

std::mutex cout_mutex;

void handle_client(int client_id) {
    std::lock_guard<std::mutex> lock(cout_mutex);    //
Locking the mutex to prevent race condition
    std::cout << "Handling client " << client_id << "
on thread " << std::this_thread::get_id() << std::endl;
}

int main() {
    const int num_clients = 5;
    std::vector<std::thread> threads;

    // Simulate handling multiple clients
    for (int i = 1; i <= num_clients; ++i) {
        threads.push_back(std::thread(handle_client,
i));
    }

    // Join all threads
    for (auto& t : threads) {
        t.join();
    }

    std::cout << "All clients handled!" << std::endl;

    return 0;
```

}

Explanation:

- The `handle_client` function simulates handling a client request. It locks the `cout_mutex` to ensure that the `std::cout` output is thread-safe, preventing multiple threads from printing to the console at the same time.
- The main thread creates several client-handling threads, each representing a client connection.
- The `join()` method ensures that the main thread waits for all client threads to finish before printing "All clients handled!" and exiting the program.

Best Practices for Managing Concurrency in Performance-Critical Applications

Managing concurrency in performance-critical applications requires careful design and attention to several key aspects:

1. **Minimize Lock Contention**:
   - Excessive locking and unlocking of mutexes can degrade performance, especially when many threads contend for the same resource. Aim to minimize the scope of critical sections (the code that needs to be protected by a lock) to reduce contention.

- o Use `std::lock_guard` or `std::unique_lock` to ensure locks are acquired and released properly, avoiding potential deadlocks.

2. **Avoid Deadlocks**:
    - o A **deadlock** occurs when two or more threads are waiting for each other to release resources, causing the program to freeze.
    - o To avoid deadlocks, always acquire locks in a consistent order, and use techniques like **timeout-based locking** or **try-locking** to prevent threads from waiting indefinitely.

3. **Use Thread Pools**:
    - o Rather than creating a new thread for every task, consider using a **thread pool** where a fixed number of threads are created upfront, and tasks are assigned to these threads as needed. This can significantly improve the efficiency of thread management in highly concurrent applications.
    - o There are libraries like **Intel Threading Building Blocks (TBB)** or **Boost** that provide thread pool implementations.

4. **Limit Thread Creation**:

o Creating too many threads can lead to overhead from context switching and resource contention. It's important to limit the number of threads to match the number of available CPU cores or use a thread pool to manage the threads efficiently.

5. **Use Atomic Operations When Possible**:

    o If you need to share data between threads and you don't need full locking, consider using **atomic operations**. C++ provides atomic types ($std::atomic$) that can be used for simple operations like incrementing or modifying values without locking.

6. **Consider Thread Safety**:

    o Ensure that shared data is accessed in a thread-safe manner. If a piece of data is shared between multiple threads, use mutexes, atomic types, or other synchronization mechanisms to avoid data races.

7. **Profile and Optimize**:

    o Always profile the performance of your multithreaded code using tools like $gprof$ or **Valgrind** to identify bottlenecks.

    o Focus on optimizing sections of the code that consume the most time and resources, such as excessive synchronization or tasks that could be parallelized more efficiently.

Summary

In this chapter, we explored the key concepts of **multithreading** and **concurrency** in C++. We learned how to use `std::thread` to create threads, `std::mutex` for mutual exclusion, and `std::condition_variable` for synchronizing thread execution. We then applied these concepts to build a simple multi-threaded server that handles multiple client connections concurrently. Finally, we discussed best practices for managing concurrency in performance-critical applications, such as minimizing lock contention, avoiding deadlocks, using thread pools, and optimizing thread management for better performance. Mastering these concurrency tools is essential for building scalable and efficient applications in C++.

Chapter 20: Testing and Debugging in Python, JavaScript, and C++

Writing Unit Tests in Python, JavaScript, and C++

Testing is an essential part of software development. Unit testing ensures that individual components of your code work as expected. Writing unit tests in Python, JavaScript, and C++ allows you to catch bugs early, ensure code quality, and improve maintainability. This chapter covers how to write unit tests in these three languages, the importance of debugging, and tools to make the process efficient.

1. Writing Unit Tests in Python

Python provides an excellent built-in library for unit testing called `unittest`, which is inspired by JUnit in Java. The `unittest` module helps you create and run tests for your code in a structured manner.

1. **Setting Up Unit Tests in Python**: A unit test typically consists of a set of tests that check individual functions or methods. The tests are usually organized into test cases, which are derived from `unittest.TestCase`.

   Example:

   ```python
   import unittest
   ```

```python
def add(a, b):
    return a + b


class TestMathOperations(unittest.TestCase):
    def test_add(self):
        self.assertEqual(add(2, 3), 5)
        self.assertEqual(add(-1, 1), 0)
        self.assertEqual(add(0, 0), 0)


if __name__ == '__main__':
    unittest.main()
```

Explanation:

- The function `add(a, b)` is the code we are testing.
- The test case `TestMathOperations` has a method `test_add` that checks if `add(a, b)` returns the correct result.
- The `assertEqual` method is used to assert that the return value matches the expected value.
- Running this script will run the tests and show the result.

2. **Running the Tests**: To run the tests, save the script as `test_math.py` and execute it from the terminal:

```bash
python test_math.py
```

2. Writing Unit Tests in JavaScript

JavaScript also has various testing frameworks, but one of the most popular is **Jest**, developed by Facebook. Jest is a powerful testing framework that makes it easy to write tests for your JavaScript code.

1. **Setting Up Unit Tests in JavaScript with Jest**: To get started with Jest, you need to install it via npm:

   bash

   ```bash
   npm install --save-dev jest
   ```

   You can then write unit tests for your JavaScript functions.

   Example:

   javascript

   ```javascript
   // math.js
   function add(a, b) {
       return a + b;
   }

   module.exports = add;
   ```

   javascript

   ```javascript
   // math.test.js
   const add = require('./math');

   test('adds 2 + 3 to equal 5', () => {
       expect(add(2, 3)).toBe(5);
   ```

```
});

test('adds -1 + 1 to equal 0', () => {
    expect(add(-1, 1)).toBe(0);
});
```

Explanation:

- o `math.js` contains the function we want to test.
- o `math.test.js` contains the test cases that check if the `add` function works correctly.
- o The `expect().toBe()` method is used to assert that the result matches the expected value.

2. **Running the Tests**: To run the tests with Jest, simply run the following command:

```bash
bash
```

```
npx jest
```

3. Writing Unit Tests in C++

In C++, we can use the **Google Test Framework (gtest)** to write and run unit tests. Google Test is a widely used library that provides robust support for unit testing in C++.

1. **Setting Up Google Test**: You need to download and install Google Test first, either by using package managers like `apt` or `brew`, or by cloning the repository from GitHub and building it manually.

Once installed, you can begin writing unit tests.

Example:

cpp

```cpp
#include <gtest/gtest.h>

int add(int a, int b) {
    return a + b;
}

TEST(MathOperations, Add) {
    EXPECT_EQ(add(2, 3), 5);
    EXPECT_EQ(add(-1, 1), 0);
    EXPECT_EQ(add(0, 0), 0);
}

int main(int argc, char **argv) {
    ::testing::InitGoogleTest(&argc, argv);
    return RUN_ALL_TESTS();
}
```

Explanation:

- The function `add(int a, int b)` is tested using the Google Test framework.
- The `TEST` macro defines a test case, where the first parameter is the name of the test suite, and the second is the test name.

- o The `EXPECT_EQ` macro is used to assert that the function returns the expected value.
- o `RUN_ALL_TESTS()` runs all tests defined in the program.

2. **Running the Tests**: To compile and run the tests, use the following commands:

```bash
bash

g++ -std=c++11 -isystem /path/to/gtest/include -pthread                              your_test_file.cpp
/path/to/gtest/libgtest.a -o test_program
./test_program
```

Introduction to Debugging Techniques for Each Language

Debugging is an essential part of software development, helping you identify and fix issues in your code. Each programming language offers various debugging techniques and tools:

1. Debugging in Python

In Python, you can use built-in tools like **pdb** (Python Debugger) to step through code and inspect variables.

1. **Using pdb**:

```python
python

import pdb
```

```
def add(a, b):
    pdb.set_trace()   # Start debugger here
    return a + b

add(2, 3)
```

Explanation:

- The `set_trace()` function pauses the execution of the program and opens an interactive debugger session. You can step through the code, inspect variables, and control the flow.

2. **Using IDEs for Debugging**:
   - Integrated Development Environments (IDEs) like **PyCharm** and **VSCode** offer visual debugging tools, such as breakpoints and variable watches, which make debugging easier.

2. Debugging in JavaScript

JavaScript offers several ways to debug code, including using **console.log()** statements and browser developer tools.

1. **Using Console.log()**:
   - The most basic form of debugging in JavaScript is using `console.log()` to output values of variables or expressions at various points in your code.

```javascript
function add(a, b) {
    console.log('Adding:', a, b);   // Log input
values
    return a + b;
}
```

2. **Using Browser Developer Tools**:

   o All modern browsers (Chrome, Firefox, etc.) come with built-in **developer tools** that provide powerful debugging features, including setting breakpoints, inspecting variables, and stepping through code.

3. Debugging in C++

C++ also has many debugging tools, and the most widely used one is **gdb** (GNU Debugger).

1. **Using gdb**:

   o To debug a C++ program with gdb, compile it with debugging symbols (-g flag):

```bash
g++ -g your_program.cpp -o your_program
```

   o Then, run it with gdb:

```bash
bash

gdb ./your_program
```

- o You can set breakpoints, step through the code, inspect variables, and control the execution flow.

2. **Using IDEs for Debugging**:
    - o **Visual Studio**, **CLion**, and **Eclipse** are popular IDEs for C++ that provide integrated debugging tools with breakpoints, call stacks, and variable watches.

Real-World Example: Writing Test Cases for a Python Application

Let's say we have a Python application that performs various mathematical operations, and we want to write test cases for it.

Example:

```python
python

def multiply(a, b):
    return a * b

def divide(a, b):
    if b == 0:
        raise ValueError("Cannot divide by zero")
    return a / b
```

1. **Writing Unit Tests**:

python

```
import unittest
from my_math import multiply, divide

class TestMathOperations(unittest.TestCase):
    def test_multiply(self):
        self.assertEqual(multiply(2, 3), 6)
        self.assertEqual(multiply(-1, 1), -1)

    def test_divide(self):
        self.assertEqual(divide(6, 2), 3)
        self.assertRaises(ValueError, divide, 6, 0)

if __name__ == '__main__':
    unittest.main()
```

Explanation:

- The `test_multiply` method checks that the `multiply` function returns the correct results.
- The `test_divide` method checks that the `divide` function works and raises a `ValueError` when attempting to divide by zero.

2. **Running the Tests**: To run the tests, save the script and execute:

```bash
bash
```

```
python test_my_math.py
```

Tools and Frameworks for Efficient Testing and Debugging

1. **Python**:
   - **unittest**: A built-in framework for writing and running tests.
   - **pytest**: A powerful testing framework that makes it easy to write simple and scalable test cases.
   - **pdb**: A debugger for Python, allowing you to step through the code and inspect variables.
   - **coverage.py**: A tool for measuring code coverage during testing.

2. **JavaScript**:
   - **Jest**: A popular testing framework for JavaScript that supports mocking, spying, and coverage.
   - **Mocha**: A flexible testing framework that can be paired with other assertion libraries.
   - **Chrome Developer Tools**: Built-in debugging tools for inspecting and stepping through JavaScript code in the browser.

- o **Node.js Debugger**: A built-in debugger for debugging Node.js applications.

3. **C++**:

  - o **Google Test (gtest)**: A widely used testing framework for C++.
  - o **gdb**: A powerful debugger for C++ programs.
  - o **Valgrind**: A tool for memory debugging and leak detection in C++ programs.

Summary

In this chapter, we learned how to write unit tests in Python, JavaScript, and C++ using frameworks like `unittest`, Jest, and Google Test. We also explored debugging techniques, such as using `pdb`, `console.log()`, and `gdb`, to find and resolve issues in code. Finally, we demonstrated a real-world example of writing test cases for a Python application. Efficient testing and debugging are essential skills for maintaining and improving the quality of software, and mastering these tools will help you build more reliable, maintainable code.

Chapter 21: Building Cross-Platform Applications

How to Create Cross-Platform Applications Using Python, JavaScript, and C++

Cross-platform applications allow developers to write code that runs on multiple operating systems (OS) such as Windows, macOS, and Linux, without needing to rewrite the code for each platform. With the growing demand for applications that can run seamlessly across different devices and OSes, cross-platform development has become an essential skill.

This chapter will explore how to create cross-platform applications using **Python**, **JavaScript**, and **C++**, and provide insight into popular frameworks such as **Electron**, **Qt**, and **React Native**. We will also go over best practices for handling cross-platform compatibility to ensure smooth and efficient development.

Creating Cross-Platform Applications in Python, JavaScript, and C++

1. **Python for Cross-Platform Applications**: Python is a popular choice for building cross-platform applications because of its simplicity and extensive ecosystem. With Python, you can leverage several libraries and frameworks

to create GUI (Graphical User Interface) applications that work across different operating systems.

- o **Tkinter**: Python's standard library for creating GUI applications. It's lightweight and works well for simple desktop applications.
- o **PyQt or PySide**: These are Python bindings for the Qt framework, which is widely used for creating robust, full-featured cross-platform applications.
- o **Kivy**: A framework for building multi-touch applications. It's cross-platform and works on Windows, macOS, Linux, and mobile platforms.

Example: A simple cross-platform Python app using Tkinter:

```python
import tkinter as tk

def greet():
    label.config(text="Hello,     Cross-Platform
World!")

root = tk.Tk()
root.title("Cross-Platform App")

label = tk.Label(root, text="Click the button
below")
```

```
label.pack(pady=20)

button = tk.Button(root, text="Click Me",
command=greet)
button.pack(pady=20)

root.mainloop()
```

- o In this example, we create a basic Tkinter window with a label and a button. This code works on all major operating systems.

2. **JavaScript for Cross-Platform Applications**: JavaScript, combined with frameworks like **Electron** and **React Native**, is a great choice for building cross-platform applications, especially for desktop and mobile apps.

   - o **Electron**: A popular framework that allows you to build desktop applications using web technologies (HTML, CSS, JavaScript). Electron apps work on Windows, macOS, and Linux.

   - o **React Native**: A framework for building mobile applications using React. It allows you to write native apps for Android and iOS using JavaScript.

   - o **Node.js**: For backend functionality, Node.js can also be used in combination with Electron or

React Native to manage APIs, databases, and other backend services.

Example: A simple Electron app:

```javascript
const { app, BrowserWindow } = require('electron')

let mainWindow

function createWindow() {
  mainWindow = new BrowserWindow({
    width: 800,
    height: 600,
    webPreferences: {
      nodeIntegration: true
    }
  })

  mainWindow.loadURL('https://example.com')
}

app.whenReady().then(() => {
  createWindow()

  app.on('activate', () => {
    if (BrowserWindow.getAllWindows().length === 0) createWindow()
```

```
  })
})

app.on('window-all-closed', () => {
  if (process.platform !== 'darwin') app.quit()
})
```

- o This Electron example creates a cross-platform desktop app that displays a webpage. It can be packaged and run on multiple operating systems.

3. **C++ for Cross-Platform Applications**: C++ is known for its performance and system-level capabilities. When building cross-platform applications in C++, using a framework like **Qt** or **wxWidgets** is common.

   - o **Qt**: A powerful C++ framework for building cross-platform applications with a wide range of features, including GUI development, networking, and more.

   - o **wxWidgets**: Another C++ framework for creating native-looking applications on multiple platforms.

Example: A simple Qt application in C++:

cpp

```cpp
#include <QApplication>
#include <QPushButton>

int main(int argc, char *argv[]) {
    QApplication app(argc, argv);

    QPushButton         button("Hello,         Cross-
Platform!");
    button.resize(200, 100);
    button.show();

    return app.exec();
}
```

- o This Qt example creates a simple window with a button labeled "Hello, Cross-Platform!" that can be compiled and run on Windows, macOS, and Linux.

Introduction to Frameworks: Electron, Qt, and React Native

1. **Electron**:
   - o Electron allows you to build cross-platform desktop applications using web technologies such as HTML, CSS, and JavaScript. It uses Chromium and Node.js to run the app on all platforms, making it easy to develop for desktop while using web technologies.

o It's ideal for building applications like Slack, Visual Studio Code, and WhatsApp Desktop.

Benefits:

o Uses web technologies (HTML, CSS, JavaScript), so web developers can easily transition to desktop development.
o Single codebase for all platforms.

Limitations:

o Electron apps tend to be large in size, and there can be performance overhead because each app runs an embedded browser (Chromium).

2. **Qt**:

o Qt is a cross-platform C++ framework that provides tools for building both desktop and mobile applications. It includes tools for GUI development, as well as support for networking, databases, and more.
o Qt applications can run on Windows, macOS, Linux, Android, and iOS.

Benefits:

- o A rich set of libraries and tools for developing full-featured applications.
- o Native look and feel for cross-platform applications.

Limitations:

- o A steeper learning curve compared to other frameworks, especially for beginners in C++.

3. **React Native**:
   - o React Native is a popular JavaScript framework for building native mobile apps for iOS and Android. It allows developers to use the same codebase to target both platforms.
   - o React Native apps are not web apps but are truly native, with performance close to that of apps written in Java or Swift.

Benefits:

- o Fast development with a single codebase for both iOS and Android.
- o Can access native device APIs for performance-critical tasks.

Limitations:

    o   Requires knowledge of platform-specific native code (e.g., Swift for iOS, Java for Android) for advanced functionality.

Real-World Example: Developing a Cross-Platform Desktop Application

Let's develop a simple cross-platform desktop application that uses **Electron** to create a text editor with basic functionality like opening and saving files.

1. **Setting Up Electron**: First, initialize a new Electron project:

bash

```
npm init -y
npm install electron --save-dev
```

2. **Create the Main Electron File** (main.js):

javascript

```
const { app, BrowserWindow, dialog } =
require('electron')
const path = require('path')

let mainWindow

function createWindow() {
  mainWindow = new BrowserWindow({
```

```
    width: 800,
    height: 600,
    webPreferences: {
      nodeIntegration: true
    }
  })

  mainWindow.loadFile('index.html')

  mainWindow.on('closed', () => {
    mainWindow = null
  })
}

app.whenReady().then(() => {
  createWindow()

  app.on('activate', () => {
    if (BrowserWindow.getAllWindows().length ===
0) createWindow()
  })
})

app.on('window-all-closed', () => {
  if (process.platform !== 'darwin') app.quit()
})
```

3. **Create the HTML Interface** (`index.html`):

```html
html
```

```html
<!DOCTYPE html>
<html lang="en">
<head>
  <meta charset="UTF-8">
  <meta name="viewport" content="width=device-width, initial-scale=1.0">
  <title>Cross-Platform Text Editor</title>
</head>
<body>
  <h1>Text Editor</h1>
  <textarea id="editor" rows="20" cols="60"></textarea>
  <button id="saveBtn">Save</button>
  <button id="openBtn">Open</button>

  <script>
    const { dialog } = require('electron')
    const fs = require('fs')
```

```javascript
document.getElementById('saveBtn').addEventListener('click', () => {
    const content = document.getElementById('editor').value
    dialog.showSaveDialog({
      title: 'Save Text File',
      defaultPath: 'text.txt',
      filters: [{ name: 'Text Files', extensions: ['txt'] }]
    }).then(result => {
      if (!result.canceled) {
```

```
            fs.writeFile(result.filePath, content,
    (err) => {
            if (err) throw err
            alert('File saved!')
        })
        }
    })
  })


document.getElementById('openBtn').addEventList
ener('click', () => {
    dialog.showOpenDialog({
      properties: ['openFile'],
      filters:    [{    name:    'Text    Files',
extensions: ['txt'] }]
      }).then(result => {
        if (!result.canceled) {
          fs.readFile(result.filePaths[0],
'utf8', (err, data) => {
            if (err) throw err

document.getElementById('editor').value = data
          })
        }
      })
    })
  </script>
</body>
</html>
```

4. **Running the Application**: Add a start script in your `package.json`:

```json
json

"scripts": {
  "start": "electron ."
}
```

Now, run the application with:

```bash
bash

npm start
```

This Electron app is a simple text editor that allows you to open and save text files. It runs on Windows, macOS, and Linux, thanks to the cross-platform nature of Electron.

Best Practices for Handling Cross-Platform Compatibility

1. **Test on Multiple Platforms**:
   o Always test your application on different operating systems to identify platform-specific issues (e.g., file paths, UI rendering, OS-specific features).

2. **Use Platform-Agnostic APIs**:
   o When possible, rely on platform-agnostic libraries and APIs (like Electron, Qt, or React Native) that abstract away OS-specific details.

3. **Handle File Paths Carefully**:
   - Different OSs use different file path separators (\ for Windows and / for Unix-based systems). Ensure that your app handles file paths correctly using platform-specific methods (`path.join()` in Node.js, `os.path` in Python).

4. **Optimize for Different Screen Sizes**:
   - Different devices and operating systems may have varying screen sizes and resolutions. Use responsive design techniques (for desktop or mobile applications) to ensure your app looks good on all screens.

5. **Check for OS-Specific Permissions**:
   - Certain features may require specific permissions on different operating systems (e.g., accessing the filesystem, network, or hardware). Be sure to handle these permissions appropriately.

Summary

In this chapter, we explored how to build cross-platform applications using **Python, JavaScript (Electron)**, and **C++ (Qt)**. We looked at the frameworks that make it easier to create cross-platform desktop and mobile applications and discussed the best practices for handling compatibility across different operating systems. By leveraging these tools and following the guidelines provided, you can create robust, user-friendly applications that work seamlessly across multiple platforms.

Chapter 22: Security Best Practices for Python, JavaScript, and C++

Common Security Vulnerabilities and How to Avoid Them

Security vulnerabilities are common in many applications, and they can lead to significant issues such as unauthorized access, data breaches, and damage to reputation. Understanding and preventing common vulnerabilities in your code is critical. Below are some of the most prevalent security vulnerabilities and how to mitigate them.

1. **SQL Injection (SQLi):**
   - **Description**: SQL injection occurs when an attacker injects malicious SQL queries into input fields, which can manipulate the SQL database and perform unintended actions (e.g., retrieving sensitive data, modifying records, or deleting data).
   - **Prevention**: Use prepared statements or parameterized queries to avoid directly including user input in SQL queries.

   Example:

   - In Python, using **SQLite** with parameterized queries:

```
python

import sqlite3

conn = sqlite3.connect('database.db')
cursor = conn.cursor()

# Vulnerable to SQL injection (don't use this!)
cursor.execute(f"SELECT * FROM users WHERE
username = '{username}' AND password =
'{password}'")

# Secure query using parameterized statements
cursor.execute("SELECT * FROM users WHERE
username = ? AND password = ?", (username,
password))
```

2. **Cross-Site Scripting (XSS)**:

   o **Description**: XSS vulnerabilities allow attackers to inject malicious scripts into web pages that are then executed by other users' browsers. This can lead to stealing session cookies, manipulating DOM elements, or redirecting users to malicious websites.

   o **Prevention**: Sanitize and escape user input properly, especially when embedding user-provided content in HTML, JavaScript, or URLs.

Example:

- In JavaScript, you can prevent XSS by escaping user input:

javascript

```
// Vulnerable to XSS (don't use this!)
document.getElementById('message').innerHTML   =
userInput;

// Secure approach: escape user input
const escapeHTML = (str) => {
    return str.replace(/&/g, '&amp;')
              .replace(/</g, '&lt;')
              .replace(/>/g, '&gt;')
              .replace(/"/g, '&quot;')
              .replace(/'/g, '&#x27;')
              .replace(/`/g, '&#x60;');
};
document.getElementById('message').innerHTML   =
escapeHTML(userInput);
```

3. **Cross-Site Request Forgery (CSRF)**:
   - **Description**: CSRF attacks involve tricking a user into performing an action on a web application without their consent, such as submitting a form or making a request on their behalf.

- o **Prevention**: Use anti-CSRF tokens, ensure that each state-changing request is protected by a unique token that is checked on the server.

4. **Insecure Deserialization**:
   - o **Description**: This occurs when data from an untrusted source is deserialized and executed without validation, allowing attackers to execute arbitrary code or manipulate application behavior.
   - o **Prevention**: Use safe serialization formats, validate all input before deserialization, and use secure libraries for handling serialized data.

5. **Buffer Overflow**:
   - o **Description**: A buffer overflow occurs when more data is written to a buffer than it can hold, leading to overwriting of adjacent memory. This can allow attackers to execute arbitrary code.
   - o **Prevention**: Use modern languages like Python or JavaScript that handle memory management automatically, or ensure that your C++ code checks bounds and avoids unsafe functions.

Implementing Encryption and Secure Communication in Python, JavaScript, and C++

1. **Encryption in Python**:
   - Python provides libraries like **PyCryptodome** and **cryptography** for implementing encryption. You can use symmetric encryption (AES) for securing data at rest or public-key encryption (RSA) for securing communications.

   Example: Encrypting data using AES in Python with the **cryptography** library:

   python

```python
from      cryptography.hazmat.primitives.ciphers
import Cipher, algorithms, modes
from      cryptography.hazmat.backends      import
default_backend

key = b'16-byte-long-key'  # 16 bytes for AES-
128
iv = b'16-byte-initial-vector'  # Initialization
vector

cipher     =     Cipher(algorithms.AES(key),
modes.CBC(iv), backend=default_backend())
encryptor = cipher.encryptor()

plaintext = b"Sensitive data"
ciphertext  =  encryptor.update(plaintext)  +
encryptor.finalize()
```

```
print("Encrypted:", ciphertext)
```

2. **Encryption in JavaScript**:

    o In JavaScript, you can use the **Web Crypto API** to perform encryption and hashing in the browser.

    Example: Encrypting data using AES-GCM with the Web Crypto API:

    javascript

```
const data = new TextEncoder().encode("Sensitive data");
const key = await crypto.subtle.generateKey(
    { name: "AES-GCM", length: 256 },
    true,
    ["encrypt", "decrypt"]
);

const iv = crypto.getRandomValues(new Uint8Array(12));

const encrypted = await crypto.subtle.encrypt(
    { name: "AES-GCM", iv: iv },
    key,
    data
);
console.log("Encrypted:", new Uint8Array(encrypted));
```

3. **Encryption in C++:**

   o In C++, you can use libraries like **OpenSSL** for implementing encryption algorithms.

Example: Using OpenSSL to encrypt data with AES:

cpp

```cpp
#include <openssl/aes.h>
#include <openssl/rand.h>
#include <iostream>

void encrypt_data(const unsigned char *key, const unsigned char *data, unsigned char *encrypted_data) {
    AES_KEY aes_key;
    AES_set_encrypt_key(key, 128, &aes_key);
    AES_encrypt(data, encrypted_data, &aes_key);
}

int main() {
    unsigned char key[16] = "thisisaverysecret";
    unsigned char data[16] = "Sensitive data";
    unsigned char encrypted_data[16];

    encrypt_data(key, data, encrypted_data);
    std::cout << "Encrypted data: ";
    for (int i = 0; i < 16; i++) {
        std::cout << std::hex << (int) encrypted_data[i];
```

```
    }
    std::cout << std::endl;

    return 0;
}
```

Real-World Example: Securing User Data in a Web Application
Let's say we are building a web application where users can register and log in. We need to secure sensitive data like passwords and ensure that communication between the client and server is encrypted.

1. **Hashing Passwords**:

   o Instead of storing passwords in plaintext, hash them using a strong hashing algorithm (e.g., bcrypt, Argon2) and store the hashed values.

   Python Example:

```python
from cryptography.hazmat.primitives import hashes
from cryptography.hazmat.primitives.kdf.pbkdf2 import PBKDF2HMAC
from cryptography.hazmat.backends import default_backend
import os
```

```
def hash_password(password: str):
    salt = os.urandom(16)
    kdf = PBKDF2HMAC(
        algorithm=hashes.SHA256(),
        length=32,
        salt=salt,
        iterations=100000,
        backend=default_backend()
    )
    return kdf.derive(password.encode())


# Hash a user's password
hashed_password                             =
hash_password("my_secret_password")
```

2. **Encrypting Communication (HTTPS)**:
   - Always use **HTTPS** (HyperText Transfer Protocol Secure) to encrypt communication between the client and the server. This can be achieved by obtaining an SSL/TLS certificate and configuring it on the server.

3. **Session Management**:
   - Use secure cookies and token-based authentication (e.g., JWT) to manage user sessions. Always set the `HttpOnly` and `Secure` flags for cookies to prevent client-side scripts from accessing them.

JavaScript Example (for setting secure cookies):

```javascript
javascript

document.cookie = "sessionToken=abc123; Secure;
HttpOnly; SameSite=Strict";
```

How to Safeguard Your Applications from Common Attacks (SQL Injection, XSS, etc.)

1. **SQL Injection (SQLi):**
   o **Best Practice**: Always use prepared statements or parameterized queries. Avoid directly concatenating user input into SQL queries.
   o **Example**: In Python, use parameterized queries with `sqlite3` or `psycopg2` for PostgreSQL.

2. **Cross-Site Scripting (XSS):**
   o **Best Practice**: Sanitize and escape user inputs before rendering them in the HTML document. Use libraries or functions that automatically escape input (e.g., `htmlspecialchars` in PHP, `escape()` in Django, or `encodeHTML` in JavaScript).

3. **Cross-Site Request Forgery (CSRF):**
   o **Best Practice**: Use anti-CSRF tokens in forms to ensure that requests are coming from legitimate users. Many frameworks (e.g.,

Django, Flask) provide built-in support for CSRF protection.

4. **Man-in-the-Middle (MITM) Attacks**:
   - **Best Practice**: Always use HTTPS to encrypt data transmitted between the client and server to prevent attackers from intercepting sensitive information.

5. **Insecure Deserialization**:
   - **Best Practice**: Always validate and sanitize input before deserializing it. Avoid using untrusted sources for deserialization, and use secure serialization formats like JSON or XML with proper validation.

Summary

In this chapter, we discussed the importance of security in software development and covered common security vulnerabilities, including SQL injection, XSS, and CSRF. We also explored how to implement encryption and secure communication in Python, JavaScript, and C++, and showed how to secure user data in a web application. By following best practices for security and using the appropriate libraries and techniques, developers can protect their applications from common attacks and ensure the integrity and confidentiality of user data.

Chapter 23: Cloud Development and Serverless Architectures

Introduction to Cloud Computing and Serverless Architectures

Cloud computing has revolutionized the way developers build and deploy applications. Traditionally, developers had to manage their own physical servers, set up and maintain infrastructure, and handle scalability. Cloud computing abstracts much of this complexity by offering on-demand infrastructure, platforms, and services via the internet. Popular cloud providers like **AWS**, **Microsoft Azure**, and **Google Cloud** provide powerful solutions that enable developers to focus on building applications without worrying about managing servers.

Serverless architectures are a cloud computing model where developers do not need to manage the server infrastructure. Instead of provisioning and maintaining servers, developers write individual functions that are executed in response to events (such as HTTP requests, database changes, or file uploads). These functions are run in stateless, event-driven environments that automatically scale based on demand. This results in a more cost-effective and scalable approach to application development.

1. **Cloud Computing Models**:

- o **Infrastructure as a Service (IaaS)**: Cloud providers offer virtual machines, storage, and networking resources. You manage the operating system and applications.

- o **Platform as a Service (PaaS)**: A higher level of abstraction where cloud providers manage the underlying infrastructure and runtime environment for you, and you focus on deploying applications.

- o **Software as a Service (SaaS)**: Cloud-based software solutions that are fully managed and ready for use without the need for developers to write code.

- o **Serverless**: A model where the cloud provider manages the execution of functions. You write code in the form of functions that are triggered by events.

2. **Benefits of Serverless**:

  - o **No server management**: You don't need to worry about infrastructure management, scaling, or server maintenance.

  - o **Automatic scaling**: Serverless architectures scale automatically based on demand.

- o **Cost efficiency**: You only pay for the computing resources used during function execution, which is often more cost-effective than maintaining dedicated servers.
- o **Faster development**: Developers can focus on business logic rather than server management, speeding up the development process.

Using Cloud Services Like AWS, Azure, and Google Cloud for Python, JavaScript, and C++ Apps

Cloud providers offer a variety of services to support applications written in Python, JavaScript, and C++. These services include compute resources (e.g., AWS Lambda, Azure Functions), storage services (e.g., S3, Azure Blob Storage), and database solutions (e.g., DynamoDB, Google Firestore). Below are some key services from the three major cloud providers:

1. **AWS (Amazon Web Services)**:
   - o **AWS Lambda**: Run code without provisioning or managing servers. Supports Python, JavaScript (Node.js), C++, and other languages.
   - o **Amazon S3**: Object storage service used for storing files and data.
   - o **DynamoDB**: A fully managed NoSQL database service.

o **API Gateway**: Used to expose HTTP endpoints that trigger Lambda functions.

2. **Azure**:

o **Azure Functions**: Similar to AWS Lambda, Azure Functions allows developers to run code without managing infrastructure. Supports multiple languages, including Python, JavaScript, and C++.

o **Azure Blob Storage**: Cloud storage for unstructured data like files, images, and videos.

o **Cosmos DB**: A globally distributed database service that supports multiple data models.

o **Azure Logic Apps**: Service for automating workflows and integrating with other cloud services.

3. **Google Cloud**:

o **Google Cloud Functions**: Serverless compute service for running code in response to events. Supports Python, JavaScript (Node.js), and other languages.

o **Google Cloud Storage**: Object storage service for storing and retrieving large amounts of data.

o **Firestore**: A NoSQL cloud database for storing and syncing data in real time.

o **Google Cloud Run**: Allows you to deploy and manage containers in a serverless environment.

Real-World Example: Building a Serverless Application with Node.js and AWS Lambda

Let's create a simple serverless application using **AWS Lambda** and **API Gateway**. This application will handle HTTP requests and return a greeting message.

1. **Set up AWS Lambda**:
   o First, log in to your **AWS Console** and navigate to the **Lambda** section.
   o Create a new Lambda function with Node.js runtime.
   o In the Lambda function, we'll write code that handles an HTTP request and returns a message.

   Lambda Function Code (Node.js):

   ```javascript
   exports.handler = async (event) => {
       const responseMessage = 'Hello, Serverless World!';

       const response = {
           statusCode: 200,
   ```

```
        body:       JSON.stringify({       message:
responseMessage }),
    };


    return response;
};
```

2. **Set up AWS API Gateway**:
   - Create a new **REST API** in **API Gateway** to expose the Lambda function via HTTP.
   - In the **API Gateway Console**, create a resource (e.g., /greet) and associate it with the Lambda function.
   - Deploy the API to a new stage (e.g., dev).
   - API Gateway will provide an endpoint URL to access the function.

3. **Invoke the Function**:
   - After deploying, you can access the serverless API via the URL provided by API Gateway.
   - When you visit the URL in your browser or use a tool like **Postman**, you'll receive the response from the Lambda function:

```
json


{
    "message": "Hello, Serverless World!"
```

}

4. **Scaling**:
   - The Lambda function automatically scales to handle multiple incoming requests. AWS manages the scaling behind the scenes, ensuring that the function can handle the load without manual intervention.

Best Practices for Cloud-Based Development and Scalability

When developing cloud-based applications and using serverless architectures, there are several best practices to follow to ensure that your application is secure, scalable, and cost-efficient.

1. **Use Environment Variables for Configuration**:
   - Store sensitive information such as API keys, database credentials, and other configuration details in environment variables, rather than hardcoding them in the code. Both AWS Lambda and Azure Functions provide secure ways to handle environment variables.

2. **Design for Scalability**:
   - Ensure your application can scale horizontally (across many instances) to handle increases in traffic. Serverless services like AWS Lambda automatically scale based on demand, but you

should design your application to be stateless, so each invocation is independent of others.

3. **Optimize Cold Starts**:
   o Serverless functions often experience a "cold start" delay when they haven't been called for a while. This happens because the cloud provider needs to provision resources for the function. Minimize cold starts by keeping functions small, optimizing their initialization code, and using provisioned concurrency (available in AWS Lambda) to reduce the startup time.

4. **Monitor and Log Functions**:
   o Use cloud monitoring and logging services like AWS CloudWatch, Azure Monitor, or Google Cloud Logging to track function performance and errors. Logs will help you identify bottlenecks, optimize performance, and troubleshoot issues.
   o Set up alerts for any failed invocations, latency issues, or resource usage thresholds.

5. **Implement Security Best Practices**:
   o Always follow the principle of least privilege when granting permissions. Use IAM roles and

policies in AWS to restrict access to only the necessary resources.

- o Use HTTPS endpoints to secure communication between the client and server.
- o Ensure proper validation and sanitization of user inputs to avoid security vulnerabilities like SQL injection and cross-site scripting (XSS).

6. **Optimize Costs**:

- o Serverless computing offers cost benefits, but it's important to optimize function execution time and resource usage to reduce costs. Use AWS Lambda's **Cost Explorer** or similar tools in other cloud platforms to monitor and analyze usage patterns.
- o Choose the appropriate function memory size based on performance testing. Too much memory can lead to unnecessary costs, while too little can cause performance issues.

7. **Manage Dependencies Efficiently**:

- o When developing serverless applications, be mindful of the dependencies you include. Keep dependencies small and avoid bloated libraries to reduce the cold start time and memory footprint of your functions.

8. **Use APIs and Event-Driven Architecture**:

    o   Design your serverless architecture to be event-driven. Use **Amazon S3 events**, **AWS SNS**, or **AWS SQS** to trigger Lambda functions in response to events such as file uploads, message queues, or scheduled tasks.

Summary

In this chapter, we explored the fundamentals of **cloud computing** and **serverless architectures**. We looked at how to build serverless applications using **AWS Lambda** and **API Gateway**, as well as how to leverage cloud services like AWS, Azure, and Google Cloud for Python, JavaScript, and C++ applications. We also discussed best practices for cloud-based development, such as ensuring scalability, security, and cost-efficiency. By embracing cloud and serverless technologies, developers can create scalable, flexible, and cost-effective applications that handle millions of requests without the need for managing infrastructure.

Chapter 24: Mobile App Development with Python, JavaScript, and C++

Introduction to Mobile App Development Frameworks: Kivy, React Native, and C++ SDKs

Mobile app development enables you to create applications that run on mobile devices such as smartphones and tablets. With the rise of **cross-platform frameworks**, developers can build apps that work on both **iOS** and **Android** from a single codebase, significantly reducing development time and costs. In this chapter, we will explore popular frameworks for mobile app development: **Kivy** for Python, **React Native** for JavaScript, and **C++ SDKs** for native mobile development.

1. Kivy for Python Mobile App Development

Kivy is an open-source Python framework for building multi-touch applications. It is especially suited for building mobile apps that run on Android and iOS, as well as applications that require rich graphical user interfaces and multi-touch support. Kivy is cross-platform, allowing you to run the same app on Windows, macOS, Linux, iOS, and Android.

- **Installation**: To get started with Kivy, first install it using `pip`:

    bash

```
pip install kivy
```

- **Example: Building a Simple App with Kivy**:

```python
from kivy.app import App
from kivy.uix.button import Button

class MyApp(App):
    def build(self):
        return Button(text="Hello, Kivy!")

if __name__ == '__main__':
    MyApp().run()
```

Explanation:

- This simple Kivy app displays a button with the text "Hello, Kivy!" on the screen.
- You can run this app on various platforms like Windows, macOS, Linux, and mobile devices (iOS and Android) by following the Kivy deployment process.

2. React Native for JavaScript Mobile App Development

React Native is a JavaScript framework developed by Facebook that allows you to build mobile applications using React. It enables you to write a single codebase in JavaScript that runs on both **iOS** and **Android**. React Native uses native components, providing better performance than hybrid mobile app frameworks, which use web views.

- **Installation**: First, install the React Native CLI:

```bash
bash

npm install -g react-native-cli
```
Then, initialize a new project:
```bash
bash

npx react-native init MyNewApp
```

- **Example: Building a Simple App with React Native**:

```javascript
javascript

import React from 'react';
import { View, Text, StyleSheet } from 'react-native';

const App = () => {
  return (
    <View style={styles.container}>
      <Text style={styles.text}>Hello, React Native!</Text>
    </View>
```

```
    );
  };


  const styles = StyleSheet.create({
    container: {
      flex: 1,
      justifyContent: 'center',
      alignItems: 'center',
    },
    text: {
      fontSize: 20,
    },
  });


  export default App;
```

Explanation:

- o This app simply displays a text message "Hello, React Native!" centered on the screen.
- o You can run this app on both iOS and Android simulators/emulators using the commands:

```bash
npx react-native run-android    # For Android
npx react-native run-ios        # For iOS
```

3. C++ SDKs for Native Mobile App Development

For more performance-critical applications, **C++** can be used with native SDKs to build mobile applications directly for iOS and Android. Native mobile development provides access to the full range of device features and gives you the ability to optimize performance, especially for resource-intensive apps.

- **For iOS (Objective-C or Swift)**: C++ can be integrated into iOS apps through Objective-C++ or by using **Xcode** with C++-based libraries.

- **For Android**: Android NDK (Native Development Kit) allows you to write performance-sensitive code in C++.

While using C++ directly for mobile development requires a deeper understanding of the platform-specific tools and libraries, it provides maximum control over the app's performance.

Building Simple Mobile Applications for iOS and Android

We'll now discuss how to build simple mobile applications using **React Native**, and integrate native features like the camera and GPS.

Building a To-Do List App with React Native

Let's build a simple **To-Do List App** where users can add and remove tasks.

1. **Install Dependencies**:

```bash
bash
```

```
npx react-native init TodoApp
cd TodoApp
npm install @react-navigation/native @react-
navigation/stack react-native-gesture-handler
react-native-reanimated react-native-safe-area-
context react-native-screens
```

2. **Create a Simple To-Do List Screen**:

App.js:

```javascript
import React, { useState } from 'react';
import { View, Text, Button, TextInput, FlatList,
StyleSheet } from 'react-native';

const App = () => {
  const [task, setTask] = useState('');
  const [tasks, setTasks] = useState([]);

  const addTask = () => {
    setTasks([...tasks, task]);
    setTask('');
  };

  const removeTask = (index) => {
    const newTasks = tasks.filter((_, i) => i !==
index);
    setTasks(newTasks);
  };
```

```
  return (
    <View style={styles.container}>
      <Text          style={styles.title}>To-Do
List</Text>
      <TextInput
        style={styles.input}
        value={task}
        onChangeText={setTask}
        placeholder="Enter new task"
      />
      <Button title="Add Task" onPress={addTask}
/>
      <FlatList
        data={tasks}
        renderItem={({ item, index }) => (
          <View style={styles.taskContainer}>
            <Text>{item}</Text>
            <Button  title="Remove"  onPress={()
=> removeTask(index)} />
          </View>
        )}
        keyExtractor={(item,     index)     =>
index.toString()}
      />
    </View>
  );
};

const styles = StyleSheet.create({
  container: {
```

```
    flex: 1,
    padding: 20,
  },
  title: {
    fontSize: 30,
    textAlign: 'center',
    marginBottom: 20,
  },
  input: {
    height: 40,
    borderColor: 'gray',
    borderWidth: 1,
    marginBottom: 10,
    paddingLeft: 8,
  },
  taskContainer: {
    flexDirection: 'row',
    justifyContent: 'space-between',
    alignItems: 'center',
    marginBottom: 10,
  },
});

export default App;
```

3. **Run the App**:

   o **To run the app on Android or iOS:**

   ```bash
   bash
   ```

```
npx react-native run-android
# OR
npx react-native run-ios
```

4. **Explanation**:

   o The app allows users to add tasks to the list and remove them.

   o We use `FlatList` to display the tasks efficiently.

   o Each task has a "Remove" button that removes it from the list when clicked.

Integrating Native Features: Camera and GPS

1. **Camera Integration** (React Native): You can use libraries such as **react-native-camera** to access the camera on mobile devices.

   Installation:

   ```bash
   npm install react-native-camera
   ```

   Usage:

   ```javascript
   import React from 'react';
   import { RNCamera } from 'react-native-camera';
   import { View, Text } from 'react-native';
   ```

```javascript
const CameraComponent = () => {
  return (
    <RNCamera
      style={{ flex: 1 }}
      type={RNCamera.Constants.Type.back}

flashMode={RNCamera.Constants.FlashMode.on}
    >
      <View style={{ flex: 1, justifyContent:
'center', alignItems: 'center' }}>
        <Text>Camera is ready!</Text>
      </View>
    </RNCamera>
  );
};

export default CameraComponent;
```

2. **GPS Integration** (React Native): You can use **react-native-geolocation-service** to access the device's GPS and get the current location.

Installation:

```bash
bash
```

```bash
npm install @react-native-community/geolocation
```

Usage:

```javascript
javascript
```

```
import React, { useEffect, useState } from
'react';
import { View, Text } from 'react-native';
import Geolocation from '@react-native-
community/geolocation';

const GPSComponent = () => {
  const [location, setLocation] =
useState(null);

  useEffect(() => {
    Geolocation.getCurrentPosition(
      (position) => {
        setLocation(position.coords);
      },
      (error) => console.log(error),
      { enableHighAccuracy: true }
    );
  }, []);

  return (
    <View>
      {location ? (
        <Text>Latitude: {location.latitude},
Longitude: {location.longitude}</Text>
      ) : (
        <Text>Loading location...</Text>
      )}
    </View>
  );
```

```
};

export default GPSComponent;
```

Best Practices for Mobile App Development

1. **Optimize Performance**:
   - Use **lazy loading** to load resources as needed, rather than loading everything at once.
   - Avoid blocking the UI thread for long operations (like network requests or large computations).
   - Minimize memory usage by using **image compression** and efficient data handling.

2. **Handle Device-Specific Issues**:
   - Be mindful of platform-specific features and design patterns. For example, Android uses **material design**, while iOS follows **Human Interface Guidelines**.
   - Test your app on multiple devices with different screen sizes, resolutions, and OS versions.

3. **Leverage Native Modules**:
   - When building cross-platform apps, use **native modules** to access platform-specific features like sensors, camera, GPS, etc.

4. **Implement Secure Data Handling**:

o Always encrypt sensitive data stored on the device and use **secure storage** options like **Keychain** on iOS or **Keystore** on Android.

5. **Manage Permissions Properly**:

o Always ask for permissions (camera, location, etc.) at runtime, especially on newer versions of iOS and Android that require explicit permission before accessing sensitive hardware features.

Summary

In this chapter, we explored mobile app development using **Kivy** for Python, **React Native** for JavaScript, and **C++ SDKs** for native mobile development. We discussed building a simple to-do list app with React Native, integrating native features like the camera and GPS, and following best practices for mobile app development. By leveraging these frameworks and tools, developers can create robust, scalable, and high-performance mobile apps that run seamlessly across different platforms.

Chapter 25: The Future of Programming Languages and Trends to Watch

What the Future Holds for Python, JavaScript, C++, and Other Emerging Languages

Programming languages evolve rapidly to meet the demands of new technologies and paradigms. Languages that dominate today, such as **Python**, **JavaScript**, and **C++**, will continue to play a significant role in the future, but there are also emerging languages and frameworks that are gaining traction. This chapter will explore the future of these popular languages and the trends shaping the next generation of programming.

1. **Python**:
    - Python has been one of the fastest-growing programming languages due to its simplicity, readability, and large ecosystem. It is particularly strong in **data science**, **machine learning**, **web development**, and **automation**.
    - **Future Outlook**:
        - Python's use in **AI** and **machine learning** will continue to grow with libraries like **TensorFlow**, **PyTorch**, and **scikit-learn** becoming increasingly sophisticated.

- As cloud computing and data science demand scalable, efficient workflows, Python may become more integrated with **high-performance computing** (HPC) tools and **GPU acceleration** libraries.
- Python's continued popularity in web development, thanks to frameworks like **Django** and **Flask**, will solidify its place in enterprise-level web applications and APIs.

2. **JavaScript**:
   - JavaScript is the backbone of the **web**, powering interactive user interfaces, dynamic content, and full-stack development with frameworks like **React**, **Vue.js**, and **Angular**.
   - **Future Outlook**:
     - With the rise of **single-page applications (SPAs)** and **progressive web apps (PWAs)**, JavaScript will continue to dominate frontend development.
     - The **Node.js** ecosystem will allow JavaScript to keep expanding into backend development, powering server-side applications.

- JavaScript will increasingly be used in areas beyond web development, including **mobile applications** through frameworks like **React Native** and **Ionic**, and even **IoT (Internet of Things)** with tools like **Johnny-Five**.

3. **C++**:

   o C++ remains one of the most powerful languages, especially for performance-critical applications such as **system programming**, **game development**, **embedded systems**, and **real-time applications**.

   o **Future Outlook**:

      - While newer languages may take over some of C++'s roles, its position in **game development** (with engines like **Unreal Engine**) and **performance optimization** will continue to be crucial.

      - **C++20** introduces features like **concepts**, **coroutines**, and **modules**, which will make the language more modern and efficient while retaining its low-level control.

- **C++** will continue to evolve in areas like **parallel computing** and **multi-threading**, especially with the increasing importance of **HPC** and **AI-driven applications**.

4. **Emerging Languages**:

   o **Rust**: Known for its memory safety and concurrency features, **Rust** is gaining popularity for system-level programming. It's becoming a popular alternative to C++ due to its safety features and speed.

   o **Go**: With its simplicity and concurrency model, **Go** is ideal for cloud services, microservices, and high-performance backends. It's increasingly used by companies like **Google**, **Uber**, and **Docker**.

   o **Swift**: Apple's language for iOS and macOS development, **Swift**, is expected to gain more traction, particularly as Apple continues to innovate with new hardware and platforms.

   o **Kotlin**: Kotlin has been adopted as the preferred language for Android development, and its interoperability with Java will keep it relevant in the mobile development space.

Key Trends in Programming Languages for 2025 and Beyond (AI, IoT, Blockchain)

The landscape of programming languages will be shaped by cutting-edge technologies like **Artificial Intelligence (AI)**, **Internet of Things (IoT)**, and **Blockchain**. Here's how these technologies are influencing language development and usage.

1. **AI and Machine Learning**:
   - **Python** will continue to be the dominant language for AI, **machine learning (ML)**, and **data science** due to its rich ecosystem of libraries and frameworks (e.g., **TensorFlow**, **PyTorch**, **Keras**).
   - As **AI** becomes more embedded in software development workflows, new languages or extensions to existing languages may emerge to simplify the development of **AI-driven applications**.
   - **C++** may see more use in AI applications that require low-latency, real-time processing (e.g., robotics, real-time AI models).

2. **IoT (Internet of Things)**:
   - The growth of the **Internet of Things** (IoT) will require new tools for managing a wide range of devices and networks. Languages like **C** and

C++ will continue to play a critical role in **embedded systems** and low-level hardware communication.

o **JavaScript** could become more prevalent in IoT projects through **Node.js**, where it can help manage data and devices in a centralized way.

o **Rust** is increasingly being considered for IoT applications due to its memory safety and low-overhead design, making it ideal for embedded systems where performance and safety are critical.

3. **Blockchain**:

o Blockchain technologies, including cryptocurrencies and smart contracts, are rapidly transforming the programming landscape. Languages like **Solidity** (for Ethereum smart contracts) are gaining popularity.

o Traditional languages like **JavaScript** and **Python** are also becoming widely used for developing decentralized applications (DApps) and interacting with blockchain networks (e.g., **Web3.js, web3.py**).

○ As **blockchain** technologies evolve, languages designed for secure and efficient decentralized systems, such as **Rust** (for its memory safety) and **Go** (for fast, concurrent backends), will become even more popular.

Real-World Examples of How Cutting-Edge Technologies Are Shaping the Future of Programming

1. **AI-Powered Code Generation**:
   ○ **GPT-3** and other AI models are starting to assist developers by auto-generating code, debugging, and even suggesting new code snippets.
   ○ AI-driven tools like **GitHub Copilot**, built using **OpenAI's GPT-3**, can already help developers write code faster and with fewer errors by providing context-aware code completions.

2. **IoT and Smart Homes**:
   ○ The rise of **smart home devices** and **IoT ecosystems** is heavily influencing programming languages and frameworks. Languages like **Python** are being used to develop applications that control and manage IoT devices, while **C++** and **Rust** are used for low-level programming of devices.

- o Platforms like **Google Assistant**, **Amazon Alexa**, and **Apple HomeKit** allow developers to create voice-controlled applications that interact with a range of IoT devices, and JavaScript has become a key language for building smart home apps.

3. **Blockchain Development**:
   - o Blockchain platforms like **Ethereum** and **Polkadot** are driving the use of new languages such as **Solidity** for developing smart contracts.
   - o Major corporations and governments are exploring **blockchain** for supply chain management, identity verification, and secure transactions, making it a growing area of interest for both developers and businesses.

4. **Cloud-Native Applications and Serverless Computing**:
   - o With the shift to **cloud-native** applications and serverless computing, languages like **JavaScript (Node.js)** and **Python** are being widely adopted for writing serverless functions in cloud platforms like **AWS Lambda**, **Google Cloud Functions**, and **Azure Functions**.
   - o As organizations move towards more **microservices**-based architectures, languages

that integrate well with these environments will continue to dominate, such as **Go**, **Rust**, and **Node.js**.

How to Stay Updated with Evolving Language Features and Industry Trends

Staying up-to-date with evolving programming languages and industry trends is essential for any developer. Here are some ways to keep learning:

1. **Follow Industry News and Blogs**:
    - Websites like **TechCrunch**, **Hacker News**, and **Dev.to** regularly feature articles and discussions about new technologies, frameworks, and languages.
    - Blogs from official language maintainers or communities (e.g., **Python Software Foundation Blog**, **Node.js Blog**, **C++ Foundation**) provide updates on language changes and upcoming features.

2. **Participate in Developer Communities**:
    - Join developer forums like **Stack Overflow**, **Reddit (r/programming)**, and **GitHub Discussions** to participate in conversations

around new language features, frameworks, and best practices.

o Attend developer conferences (e.g., **PyCon**, **React Conf**, **Google I/O**, **Apple WWDC**) where new technologies and language features are often announced.

3. **Explore Documentation and Release Notes**:

o Regularly review the official documentation of the languages and tools you work with to stay aware of new features, deprecations, and security updates.

o Major language updates, such as **C++20**, **Python 3.x** versions, and **ECMAScript** releases, often come with extensive changelogs that provide insight into future trends.

4. **Experiment with Emerging Technologies**:

o Actively try out emerging technologies like **AI**, **Blockchain**, and **IoT** in side projects or hackathons. This hands-on experience will not only improve your skills but also keep you ahead of industry trends.

5. **Enroll in Online Courses**:

o Platforms like **Coursera**, **Udemy**, **Pluralsight**, and **edX** offer courses on the latest trends, including new programming languages, tools, and technologies. Taking courses on **AI**, **blockchain**, and **cloud computing** will help you stay relevant.

Summary

In this chapter, we explored the future of programming languages, highlighting the ongoing evolution of **Python, JavaScript**, and **C++** alongside emerging languages like **Rust** and **Go**. We also discussed key industry trends like **AI, IoT**, and **blockchain**, and how they are shaping the future of programming. By understanding and adapting to these trends, developers can position themselves at the forefront of the rapidly changing tech landscape. Staying updated with new technologies, actively experimenting with them, and engaging with developer communities are crucial strategies for ensuring long-term success in the programming world.

Chapter 26: Summary: Becoming a Master of Modern Programming Languages

Recap of the Core Programming Languages and Their Applications

In this book, we have explored some of the most important and widely used programming languages today: **Python**, **JavaScript**, and **C++**. Each language has its unique strengths, making them suitable for specific domains. Let's quickly recap the key takeaways for each language and its primary applications:

1. **Python**:
   - **Core Strengths**: Python is known for its simplicity, readability, and vast ecosystem. It is highly popular in **data science, machine learning, web development**, and **automation**. Python's libraries like **TensorFlow, PyTorch, Django**, and **Flask** make it a go-to language for AI, web frameworks, and rapid prototyping.
   - **Use Cases**: Python is a top choice for applications in **data analysis, scientific computing, AI/ML, automation scripts**, and **backend development**.

2. **JavaScript**:

   o **Core Strengths**: JavaScript is the backbone of **web development**, with its ability to run on both the frontend (in browsers) and backend (using Node.js). It powers **dynamic web pages, SPAs (Single Page Applications)**, and **progressive web apps (PWAs)**. JavaScript's versatility extends to mobile development through frameworks like **React Native**.

   o **Use Cases**: JavaScript is essential for building **interactive websites, web applications**, and **real-time applications** (e.g., chat apps, online games). It is also used in mobile development and server-side programming via Node.js.

3. **C++**:

   o **Core Strengths**: C++ offers **high performance, low-level memory control**, and **object-oriented programming (OOP)**, making it ideal for **systems programming, game development, embedded systems**, and **real-time applications**.

   o **Use Cases**: C++ is indispensable for building **game engines** (e.g., Unreal Engine), **high-performance applications** (e.g., real-time systems, financial systems), and **embedded**

software where direct hardware access and performance are critical.

In addition to these established languages, emerging languages like **Rust**, **Go**, and **Kotlin** are becoming increasingly important in certain areas, such as **performance-oriented applications**, **concurrent programming**, and **Android development**. These languages are influencing the evolution of the programming landscape.

How to Continue Improving Your Skills in Python, JavaScript, C++, and Other Languages

Becoming a master of programming languages takes time, effort, and dedication. Here are several strategies to continue improving your skills in **Python, JavaScript, C++**, and other languages:

1. **Keep Building Projects**:
   - **Hands-on practice** is the best way to learn and retain programming concepts. Start by building projects that challenge you to apply your knowledge. For instance:
     - Build a **web application** with Python using **Flask** or **Django**.
     - Create a **real-time chat app** with JavaScript (Node.js and WebSockets).

- Develop a **performance-critical system** or **game engine** with C++.
  - Work on **open-source projects** and collaborate with other developers to gain experience and get feedback from the community.

2. **Master the Fundamentals**:
   - The fundamentals of **data structures**, **algorithms**, **design patterns**, and **object-oriented principles** are essential in every language. Regardless of the language you use, having a strong understanding of these concepts will make it easier to learn new languages and technologies.
   - Familiarize yourself with **memory management** (especially in C++), **functional programming concepts** (in Python and JavaScript), and **asynchronous programming** (in JavaScript and Python).

3. **Take Online Courses and Tutorials**:
   - Online platforms like **Coursera**, **Udemy**, **edX**, and **Pluralsight** offer comprehensive courses on specific programming languages and advanced topics. Engage in structured learning to deepen your understanding of languages.

- o Participate in coding challenges on websites like **LeetCode**, **HackerRank**, or **Codewars** to improve your problem-solving skills.

4. **Contribute to Open-Source Projects**:
   - o Contributing to **open-source** projects is a great way to learn from others, collaborate with developers worldwide, and gain real-world experience. Start by contributing to projects that interest you, and gradually tackle more complex issues.

5. **Stay Updated with Language Features**:
   - o Languages evolve, with new features and libraries being added regularly. Make sure to stay updated by reading release notes, following language-specific blogs, and joining developer communities (e.g., Stack Overflow, GitHub, Reddit).
   - o For instance, **Python** has seen major updates in recent versions (e.g., **f-strings**, **asyncio**), while **JavaScript** introduced new features like **ES6** (Arrow functions, Promises) and the upcoming **ES2022** features (class fields, top-level await).

6. **Attend Conferences and Meetups**:

- o Conferences like **PyCon, React Conf, Google I/O,** and **GDC (Game Developers Conference)** offer insights into the latest trends and advancements in the programming world. Attending these events will also help you network with professionals and keep your skills sharp.
- o Participate in **local meetups** or online communities to discuss language features, frameworks, and best practices.

7. **Learn Multiple Languages**:

- o As a developer, **learning multiple programming languages** is a huge advantage. It broadens your skillset and provides new perspectives on problem-solving. For example, learning a low-level language like **C++** can help you better understand memory management, which can inform your work in higher-level languages like Python or JavaScript.
- o Experiment with different paradigms, such as **functional programming** (in languages like **Haskell** or **Elixir**) or **concurrent programming** (in **Go** or **Rust**).

Real-World Tips from Industry Experts on Becoming a Versatile, Modern Programmer

1. **Focus on Problem-Solving, Not Just Syntax**:
   - According to many industry experts, programming is about solving problems, not just writing code. Understanding the problem and coming up with the best solution is more important than memorizing syntax.
   - Embrace a **problem-solving mindset** and approach programming as a tool to find elegant solutions to real-world challenges.

2. **Understand the Ecosystem, Not Just the Language**:
   - Learning a programming language is just the start. Understanding the entire ecosystem — including **libraries, frameworks, tools**, and **best practices** — is what makes you a proficient developer.
   - For example, learning **JavaScript** means more than just knowing how to write JavaScript code. You should understand how to use **React**, **Node.js, npm**, and how to handle asynchronous programming with Promises or async/await.

3. **Write Clean, Readable, and Maintainable Code**:

- o Writing **clean code** is a crucial skill that every developer should master. Clean code is not just about making your code work; it's about making it understandable, maintainable, and scalable.
- o Follow best practices like adhering to **SOLID principles**, writing **modular** and **reusable** code, and following **coding standards** for the language you're working with.

4. **Collaborate with Others**:
   - o The ability to collaborate effectively with others is one of the most valuable skills in modern software development. Whether it's through pair programming, code reviews, or participating in open-source projects, learning from others will help you improve faster.
   - o Working on diverse teams and with different technologies will expose you to new techniques and tools that you wouldn't encounter working alone.

5. **Learn to Embrace Change**:
   - o The programming landscape is always changing. New languages, frameworks, and paradigms emerge regularly. A successful programmer must learn to embrace these

changes, adapt quickly, and continuously evolve with the field.

- o Stay curious and open to learning new things. Don't be afraid to experiment with new languages, tools, or techniques, even if they're outside your comfort zone.

Final Thoughts on the Importance of Learning Multiple Programming Languages for the Future

In the ever-evolving tech landscape, being proficient in a single programming language is no longer enough. The most successful developers are those who can adapt to new languages and paradigms quickly, depending on the requirements of the project.

Learning multiple languages opens doors to a broader range of opportunities. Different languages are better suited for different tasks, and having the knowledge to choose the right tool for the job is essential in today's competitive software development environment. Whether it's **Python** for rapid development, **JavaScript** for web applications, or **C++** for performance optimization, understanding the strengths and weaknesses of various languages gives you the versatility to handle a wide variety of projects.

As we move towards a more **AI-driven, cloud-based**, and **IoT-connected** world, programming languages will continue to evolve.

By staying curious, embracing new technologies, and honing your skills across multiple languages, you can ensure that you remain a relevant, versatile, and successful programmer in the future.

In Summary, becoming a master of modern programming languages involves both deep expertise in specific languages and a willingness to explore and adapt to new tools and techniques. By following the strategies outlined in this book and continually improving your skills, you'll be well-equipped to tackle the challenges of tomorrow's software development world.

www.ingramcontent.com/pod-product-compliance
Lightning Source LLC
LaVergne TN
LVHW051432050326
832903LV00030BD/3049